When God Answers Your Prayers

Love you Mom,)

Diana

7/7/16

When God Answers Your Prayers

Karen O'Connor

HARVEST HOUSE PUBLISHERS
EUGENE, OREGON

Scripture quotations, unless otherwise indicated, are taken from The Holy Bible, New International Version® NIV®. Copyright © 1973, 1978, 1984, 2011 by Biblica, Inc.™ Used by permission. All rights reserved worldwide.

Verses marked NLT are taken from the *Holy Bible*, New Living Translation, copyright © 1996, 2004. Used by permission of Tyndale House Publishers, Inc., Wheaton, IL 60189 USA. All rights reserved.

Verses marked NASB are taken from the New American Standard Bible®, © 1960, 1962, 1963, 1968, 1971, 1972, 1973, 1975, 1977, 1995 by The Lockman Foundation. Used by permission. (www.Lockman.org)

Cover photo © Dugan Design Group, Bloomington, Minnesota

Cover design by Dugan Design Group, Bloomington, Minnesota

Published in association with Books & Such Literary Agency, 52 Mission Circle, Suite 122, PMB 170, Santa Rosa, CA 95409-5370, www.booksandsuch.biz.

WHEN GOD ANSWERS YOUR PRAYERS
Copyright © 2013 by Karen O'Connor
Published by Harvest House Publishers
Eugene, Oregon 97402
www.harvesthousepublishers.com

Library of Congress Cataloging-in-Publication Data
O'Connor, Karen.
When God answers your prayers / Karen O'Connor.
    p. cm.
    ISBN 978-0-7369-4840-1 (pbk.)
    ISBN 978-0-7369-4841-8 (eBook)
    1. Prayer—Christianity. 2. Prayer—Christianity—Anecdotes. I. Title.
BV220.O26 2012
242—dc23
                      2012026070

Printed in the United States of America

13 14 15 16 17 18 19 20 / BP-JH / 10 9 8 7 6 5 4 3 2 1

For Sherry Kyle, Miralee Ferrell, and Kimberly Johnson,
writing colleagues and dear friends.

Acknowledgments

I wish to thank these men and women for allowing me to interview them regarding their experiences on how God answered their prayers in the nick of time and for allowing me to create stories based on their real situations:

Rhonda Abellera • Beverly Adler • Nancy Aguilar • Ron Berry • Joseph Bentz • Renetta Butler • Tami Chelew • Dale Collins • Jon Drury • Judy Durden • Michael Ehret • Miralee Ferrell • Kristine Flynn • Charles Flowers • Gloria Hall • Debra Holmes • Kimberly Johnson • Beverly Lum • June O'Connor • Charise Olson • Joe Phillips • Marilyn Prasow • Simon Presland • Ginger Ramin • Cheryl Ritchey • Rene Schlaepfer • Anita Siriwa • Sandra Victor • James Warren • Glenda Wheeler

Contents

A Note from Karen

The Bible makes it clear that our heavenly Father hears and answers our prayers wherever we are, in whatever situation, and whenever we seek him.

> Do not be anxious about anything, but in every situation, by prayer and petition, with thanksgiving, present your requests to God. And the peace of God, which transcends all understanding, will guard your hearts and your minds in Christ Jesus (Philippians 4:6-7).

God's Word does *not*, however, say that he will answer our prayers immediately or necessarily in the manner we want or expect. We all experience times when the Lord *seems* to hold back, or looks the other way, or even refuses to communicate with us at all. We plead and beg, but still we hear no answers…or at least not the ones we're hoping for. Although as his children we should trust him with all our hearts, often we don't. We become so focused on our own points of view that we don't rest until we hear the answer *we* desire. But God may have something else in mind. Maybe…

- we need to turn our gaze on him, not on our situation.
- another detail has to be settled first.
- our thinking requires an adjustment.
- the timing isn't right for reasons unknown to us.
- he wants to stretch and mature us so we depend more on him.
- our request is selfish.
- we have unconfessed sin that is standing in the way.

Whatever the case, God is God and we are not. Ultimately, he will do what is right and good and perfect for our situation according to his will and in his timing. We can take comfort in that truth like a child trusting a parent to make the right decision or we can balk and complain and then feel ashamed for not trusting when the answer does come. As C.S. Lewis put it, "Relying on God has to start all over every day, as if nothing has yet been done."

Often, when we least expect it, at the very moment we're ready to give up, when we're sitting on the curb in tears or pacing the floor and running a hand through our hair, the phone rings with the news that our house or boat sold, or a sick child's fever broke, or a book proposal was accepted, or a job interview resulted in an offer of employment. God answers our prayers. Never too early. Never too late. Often just in the nick of time.

This was the case with my friend Cheryl Ritchey. "One day during a pouring rain, my husband and I stopped at a fast-food restaurant for coffee," she said. "When we returned to our car, the battery was dead." Cheryl had left the headlights on. "There we stood in the downpour by the side of the car, hood up, without a cell phone, trying to think of something we could do." They didn't go back into the restaurant for assistance because, as Cheryl said, "I always turn to God first." So she prayed, "Lord, please send us help."

Minutes later God's answer arrived. A large, black SUV pulled up with a lady trooper inside. She pulled into the space next to their car.

"Can I help?'" she asked.

Cheryl pointed at the engine compartment. "We have a dead battery."

The officer offered to use her cables to jump-start the battery. Soon the car was running again. While thanking the woman, Cheryl noticed the woman's large, gold nameplate pinned to her uniform. In bold black letters it read: LORD.

"Now I'd say that was an answer to prayer in the nick of time," said Cheryl. "And God even put his name on it!"

In this uplifting book, you'll find other amazing and sometimes humorous answers to the prayers of real people regarding real situations. I pray they will encourage you and boost your faith in God. He *always* hears his children, and he *always* answers...though sometimes waiting until what we consider the last possible moment.

Karen O'Connor
Watsonville, California

Hidden Love

Hatred stirs up conflict, but love covers over all wrongs.
PROVERBS 10:12

"Early in our marriage, my husband and I had a very difficult season because of a deep hurt between us," Terra shared. "My pillow was often wet with tears. I especially remember one Valentine's Day in particular. Rick walked through the front door after work carrying an enormous bouquet of red, white, and pink heart balloons. Instead of being appreciative of his thoughtfulness, I was angry. I raged at him in my mind: 'I can't believe you spent all that money! What were you thinking?' As far as I was concerned, Rick couldn't do anything right."

One weekend Terra's in-laws came to visit from another state. During their stay, Terra and Rick gave each other fake smiles and forced hugs. "We spoke nicely to each other, but it was all a facade," added Terra. "It seemed easier to pretend than to make waves. We took pictures of all of us 'being happy,' but when I look at them now, many years later, I see the sadness in our eyes. No one else knew the pain we were carrying."

Following one conflict after another, the couple gradually drifted apart. They no longer liked or respected each other. "To save face, we continued the pretense in front of others and even between ourselves." Their problems grew to the point where they could no longer hide the pain. "We started talking about divorce because it seemed like our only option."

Terra cried to God for help. She was at a loss for what else she could say or do to improve the situation. "Sometimes in desperation, I even prayed that something bad would happen to one of us, such as an accident, so we wouldn't have to go through a divorce and hurt our parents and two young sons."

Finally Terra and Rick decided to confide in their pastor so they met for counseling. They also phoned a trusted friend and small-group leader at their church. David invited them to his home to talk and pray. "He ushered us into his living room, and we sat on a sofa facing him," said Terra. "He held our hands and prayed, asking God for wisdom and for healing for our marriage. He looked up at us with sad eyes, was quiet for a moment, and then he suddenly started weeping—softly at first. Then his silent tears changed to deep, uncontrollable sobs."

The couple didn't know what to do, so they sat and watched David. "We forgot our own heartbreak for a while," Terra said, "and wondered how to comfort our friend."

Moments later he stopped crying.

"What's wrong, David?" Rick asked.

David looked at Rick and Terra with compassion. "The grief of Jesus overwhelmed me," he explained. "Jesus is weeping over your marriage."

Neither Terra nor Rick had ever heard of such a thing. They were stunned. They knew David well, and he wasn't a person given to drama or emotional outbursts. "Over the years we'd shared meals and celebrations together, gone on trips with his family, and been participants in a Bible study in his home, yet we had never seen him cry," Terra shared. "We didn't understand what had happened, yet we never doubted his explanation."

The thought of Jesus grieving over their marriage was more than the couple could handle. "Rick and I both started crying as we too caught a glimpse of God's great love for us. That night we knew—even in our brokenness—there was hope. We humbly asked God to renew our love and commitment to each other. Sometimes," Terra continued, "I think the Lord pulls back the veil here on earth and gives us a glimpse of him. That's what happened when David prayed for us."

Over the next several weeks, Terra and Rick noticed subtle changes in their relationship. "Our hearts began to soften," Terra noted. "We started to forgive each other. What surprised us most were the 'new' eyes God gave us for each other. We fell in love again. We knew the only explanation for this change was God's mercy and grace being poured into our hurting hearts. He had given us a second chance just in the nick of time.

"I learned that God 'is able to do immeasurably more than all we ask or imagine, according to his power that is at work within us' just like Ephesians 3:20 says. Though I had been taught as a child that God loves me, after this experience, I *felt* loved by God because he met me right where I was and answered my cry for help."

Since that time, Terra and Rick have realized how much they need to pay attention to their relationship—to nurture it and to keep learning and growing *together*. "Through the years since then," Terra revealed, "we've taken marriage classes, gone to retreats for couples, and sought godly counsel when we've experienced difficulties. We celebrated our thirty-fifth anniversary in June of 2011. We love being married!"

In ordinary life we hardly realize that we receive a great deal more than we give, and that it is only with gratitude that life becomes rich.
Dietrich Bonhoeffer

Dream Job

*My God will meet all your needs according to
the riches of his glory in Christ Jesus.*
PHILIPPIANS 4:19

"I was nearing the completion of my studies for a PhD," shared Joseph Bentz. "I was ready to look for a job as an English professor at a university. I knew I wanted to work at a different institution than the one where I was teaching at the time. I applied to 34 schools all over the country and prayed mightily that God would lead me to the right place."

The year before, Joe had sought a position he considered a dream job. "The school seemed interested, and I had some long telephone discussions with the dean, but the committee ended up choosing someone with a completed doctorate and more experience than I had. Their decision made sense, but I was terribly disappointed."

Joe admits that he carried that disappointment with him during his new job search. "The market for English professors was very tough at that time," he said. "And I hadn't yet completed my dissertation, so I received some rejections right away. Azusa Pacific University (APU) in Southern California was among them. I'd met the chair of the English Department at a conference and hoped he might have an opening for me. I was single then and living in Illinois. Moving to sunny Southern California sounded like a great adventure, but the door closed. I filed that rejection with the others and moved on."

When spring semester started, despite many interviews, it was apparent to Joe that he was to remain at the school where he was already employed. "God had not answered my prayers in the way I'd hoped." As he settled in and let go of his disappointment, he received an unexpected letter in the mail from the chair of the English Department at APU—four months after the man had turned down Joe's application. It turned out that one of the faculty members was stepping down so there would be an opening after all. "Are you still interested in interviewing for this position?" the man wrote.

"Was I? Absolutely! I was on an airplane the very next week. The interview went well, and by the middle of April I received a contract for the following school year." Two weeks later Joe successfully defended his dissertation for his doctorate.

"As I look back now, 20 years later, the timing of this event seems perfect. I got the job just when I needed it—in the nick of time, you might say—and everything fell into place. I still work at APU, and I have spent the most productive years of my career here. I also met my wife in California, and we now have two children."

From this experience, Joe learned that he can rarely see the significance of events at the time he's going through them. "In the present I simply have to trust God to pull me through. He always does, but in a moment of worry and confusion, I feel a little shaky, wondering why there are so many unknowns and why he is taking so long to answer." One thing Joe realized during that trial, and through many similar experiences, is to focus on what God presents in the moment instead of trying to figure out the future. "He rarely does things in the sequence I expect or uses the methods I would choose," added Joe. "But God has brought joy into my life regardless of the circumstances, so I choose to trust him to carry me the rest of the way."

Faith is all that dreamers need to see into the future.

Jim Stovall

Peace at Last

Take away the disgrace I dread,
for your laws are good.
PSALM 119:39

"I struggled mightily in prayer over my volatile relationship with my adoptive father, often with reservation and constant despair, fearing in the back of my mind there would never be relief," Owen revealed. He couldn't believe or even imagine there'd be a time when he could fully forgive his father and find true peace. "For years I felt a dull ache in the middle of my heart where he was concerned. He would have a violent temper one day and act like my best friend the next."

As Owen moved from his teenage years into early adulthood, he indulged in negative fantasies about the man. "I found myself wishing for harm and punishment to rain down on him. I was so hurt and angry I couldn't consider anything else." Through the years Owen spoke with various spiritual counselors, friends, and therapists. Each one talked with him about unconditional forgiveness, and urged him to pray for personal healing.

"My walk with God was weak," said Owen, "so my ability to forgive was poor. I didn't have the energy to move in that direction." But God was present in Owen's situation even though he didn't realize it at the time.

"Eventually God led me to a recovery path." There he received tools and information about how to restore his spiritual health. "Once again I was faced with the precept that forgiveness results in true strength. But when it came to my father, my spirit rebelled." Even so, Owen did start praying more consistently for his father and kept turning him over to the Lord. "My heart wasn't in it completely," Owen said, "but I tried." The best he could do was detach from his dad in mind and body, though those attempts were never fully successful.

"In February 2006, I received a phone call from my brother in Dallas, Texas," said Owen. "He told me our father had just passed away. The irony was that Dad lived only a few miles from where I was living at the time." Owen said he continued on with his day, trying to put the news behind him. "But a flood of memories came up, and they shook me to the core. I prayed for peace. I prayed for forgiveness. I prayed for relief. But I was stuck." Then a thought came to him. "I must pray for my father and ask for his forgiveness, nothing more and nothing less."

Owen reached out to a friend for support, and the two went to the local hospital morgue. There Owen lay prostrate before his father's body and prayed. "I asked that my dad would be in the presence of God. I asked Dad for his forgiveness for my being an angry, resentful son. I prayed for peace for my dad through eternity, and then I walked out. Within several steps I felt relief and lightness sweep over me like never before. From that day to this, whenever I think of Dad, the good far outweighs the bad."

Owen was set free from grief, anger, hatred, and fear in the nick of time. He was able to say his final goodbye with peace.

"The most important lesson I've learned about prayer is to stay the course," Owen shared. "It's never too late to pray. The timing is always right because God is working in the background even when we can't see a way out."

The Lord showed Owen the truth of the Scripture, "We know that in all things God works for the good of those who love him, who have been called according to his purpose" (Romans 8:28). Owen said, "I'd given up hope of finding peace, yet God showed me that my serenity will come when I forgive others and ask for their forgiveness—especially those I hold in contempt. Walking in prayer, sometimes one slow, painful step at a time, is still the best way."

Love begins at home and it is not how much we do…
but how much love we put in that action.

Mother Teresa

Most Beautiful One

From the depths of the earth you will again bring me up.
PSALM 71:20

For seven nights King Xerxes, a Persian who ruled in the third or fourth century BC, held a great party. On the last day of the revelry, being in high spirits from wine, he told his servants to get Queen Vashti "wearing her royal crown, in order to display her beauty to the people and nobles, for she was lovely to look at" (Esther 1:11). But when the attendants delivered the king's command, Queen Vashti refused to come. The king was "furious and burned with anger." He removed her as queen and banished her from the kingdom. Then he issued a royal decree for all the beautiful, young women in his realm to be presented to him so he could select a new queen.

Esther, a Jewish girl being raised by her cousin Mordecai following the death of her parents, caught the king's eye. He was attracted to Esther more than to any of the other young women, so he set a royal crown on her head and made her queen instead of Vashti.

Mordecai had an enemy named Haman, the king's prime minister. Haman detested Mordecai because he refused to bow down when Haman entered the palace gates. This infuriated the prime minister so much that he looked for a way to discredit Mordecai. He found one. Discovering that Mordecai was Jewish, Haman planted in the mind of King Xerxes the idea that people who were different should be executed. He said certain people refused to obey the king's laws. Unaware that his beautiful queen and her cousin would be among this group, the king agreed.

When Mordecai heard of Haman's plan, he begged Esther to do something to save her people—to beseech the king's help. If she did, however, her life would be in danger because no one was allowed to approach the king unless he summoned him or her. How hopeless she must have felt.

Esther requested prayer, and she also prayed. I imagine she spent hours in prayer because so much was on the line. Then Esther gathered her courage and entered the king's throne room. Because he loved Esther, the king stretched out his scepter and welcomed her into his presence. She invited him to a special banquet where he would be the guest of honor. She included Haman in the invitation. The two men attended the feast. Afterward, Xerxes promised Esther she could have anything she wanted—even half his kingdom. Instead, Esther invited the king and Haman to a second banquet. The king agreed once again.

Meanwhile, Haman was moving forward with his plans to murder the Jews. He ordered a stake to be erected so he could impale or hang Mordecai. But God responded in the nick of time. Haman went to the court to speak to the king to ask if Mordecai could be killed, but before he had a chance to say anything, the king told him to honor Mordecai for reporting a plot against him. Haman did as commanded, but he went home and furiously complained about it to his wife and friends. And then the king's servants came to get Haman for the second dinner Esther was hosting.

At the end of the next dinner, Xerxes again promised Esther anything she wanted. She asked that her life be spared, and her people be saved from an evil man.

The king demanded, "Who is he? Where is he—the man who has dared to do such a thing?" (Esther 7:5).

"An adversary and enemy! This vile Haman!" replied Esther. She went on to explain his plot against the Jews.

The king ordered Haman be put to death immediately on the stake he'd built to kill Mordecai.

Then the king promoted Mordecai to Haman's place and authorized Mordecai and Esther to write a decree in his name that would allow the Jews to defend themselves and to kill their enemies on the same day Haman's edict would occur. The Jews destroyed all who sought to kill them. Thousands went down, including the 10 sons of Haman.

Esther and her cousin Mordecai sent out a letter to the Jews confirming an annual commemoration—Purim—of the saving of the Jews. King Xerxes continued his reign with Queen Esther at his side, and Mordecai continued as the second most powerful man in Xerxes' kingdom.

You must do the thing you think you cannot do.

Eleanor Roosevelt

Road to Victory

Commit your way to the LORD; trust in him.
PSALM 37:5

"My husband, Denny, and I started our own business, Durden General Engineering, 35 years ago," Judy Durden said. "With God's help, I became a general engineering licensed contractor in 1987. But in 2008, when the economy took a major downturn, we faced overwhelming odds. Work became scarce, and contracts were difficult to obtain. The following three years were the hardest of all."

Judy then shared something she'd heard a pastor once say. "When you're up against a major storm in your life, you have two choices. The first is to allow it to destroy you. The second is to run to Jesus." For Judy, the choice was clear. She ran to Jesus. "As a young girl, I lived in a non-Christian home. But the Lord always had his hand on me. When I grew weary, he picked me up and carried me in his loving arms." At age nine she became a follower of Christ and has continued on that path ever since.

"I believe God allows the challenges so he can get our attention. He certainly got mine during the economic recession."

In this difficult time with the business, the Holy Spirit spoke to Judy about the power of prayer. "I was to get on my knees and humble myself before God," she said. "So every morning my husband and I knelt before the Lord, prayed together, and read Scripture."

Judy and Denny heard that some contractors were certain Durden General Engineering wouldn't survive. "But they didn't know our Master," added Judy with a twinkle in her eye. "Yes, there were times when I wanted to give up. And many mornings I lay in bed and worried. But I knew that my God was in control, and so I prayed the doubts away. I could sense victory was just around the bend."

On one particular Friday when an employee payroll was due, the business had no cash on hand. The couple needed a miracle. "I remember that morning speaking to God about our situation," said Judy, "even though I knew he knew all about it before I asked. The Holy Spirit moved me in such a way that when I picked up the mail I felt certain there'd be a check for enough to cover our expenses." And sure enough, the first envelope held a check from a contractor whose payment to the company was not due for another 10 days. "That day we met payroll and were able to pay a few bills," Judy said. "God is faithful and always on time—even when it *feels* to us like it's just in the nick of time."

Judy thanked God over and over that day for his perfect answer to her prayers. "It's easy to praise him when you're on the mountaintop," she added, "but the sacrifice of praise is when you're going through a valley. That's when your faith grows stronger. Hard times can be your best times. Jesus taught me so much about me during those difficult times."

Since that Friday, Judy and Denny have faced many more challenges, but they always turn to God in prayer. "He taught me to speak to him every day and to trust him in all things," Judy shared. "He showed me that in surrendering all of me I please him because that's what he's always wanted!

"He has blessed my husband and me more than I can say. Our greatest blessings are our three sons and their wives, our seven grandchildren, and our great-granddaughter. God gives blessings to everyone who turns to him."

When you fail, you learn from the mistakes you made,
and it motivates you to work even harder.
Natalie Gulbis

A Little Extra

Teach me your way, LORD;
lead me in a straight path because of my oppressors.
PSALM 27:11

Between college semesters, a friend in Utah offered Dale a job building homes. He took it, even though it meant delaying going back to classes for a few months. "I remember enjoying the varieties of scenic beauty as I drove from the Columbia River Gorge region of Washington and Oregon to Salt Lake City, as well as seeing the Great Salt Lake and the surrounding snow-capped mountains." This area would be his new home for the time he held the job.

Several months later, when Dale was ready to return to school, he started the drive back to the Columbia Gorge, only to make a startling discovery. "I'd forgotten to fill my gas tank before I left. There I was in wide-open country miles from any city, and the gas gauge hit the empty mark. Instantly my body tensed." Dale hadn't seen a car or a building for miles, and he couldn't see any up ahead either. "Fear of being stranded in unknown territory motivated me to keep going," he said, "but at a slower, gas-saving speed."

At the time, Dale was a young believer, but he knew enough to start praying immediately for God's help. "I was desperate," he added, "so when I felt deep anxiety overwhelm me, I began singing my favorite church songs. I questioned whether God would hear my prayer or even if he cared about me, but he was my only hope so I continued to trust, pray, and sing.

"Miles later—I'm not sure how many—I spotted what appeared to be a country store and gas station in the distance. That gave me some relief, but still I couldn't be sure of what I was seeing until I arrived." Dale coasted into the driveway, filled up, and paid the clerk. "Then I looked at the receipt, noting that I'd pumped one gallon more than the tank was supposed to hold!" He let out a great sigh of thanks. "I realized then that by giving me 'just a little bit more,' God was showing me that it really was his loving care that enabled me to reach the gas station in the nick of time."

That experience confirmed for Dale "that God is ever-present and does care about people." He said, "I didn't look at this experience as a 'lesson.' I was just thankful. As I continued my journey, I sang praises to God off and on with a grateful heart."

Humor is to life what shock absorbers are to automobiles.
Stan Toler

The real problem of the Christian life comes where people do not usually look for it. It comes the very moment you wake up each morning. All your wishes and hopes for the day rush at you like wild animals. And the first job each morning consists simply in shoving them all back; in listening to that other voice, taking that other point of view, letting that other larger, stronger, quieter life come flowing in. And so on, all day. Standing back from all your natural fussings and frettings; coming in out of the wind.

C.S. Lewis, *Mere Christianity*

Split-Second Grace

No harm will overtake you, no disaster will come near your tent. For he will command his angels concerning you to guard you in all your ways.

PSALM 91:10-11

Brenda and her husband, Brad, worked until sweat ran down their faces as they replaced dry, rotted overhead beams in the damp basement of their newly purchased home in Sierra Creek, California. "High atop our ladders we stood with construction belts strapped to our waists. We wrestled with the beams using crowbars and hammers," Brenda said.

"I'd wrapped our five-month-old son, Patrick, warm and tight in blankets. He was asleep in his car seat on the floor a good distance to the left side of my ladder and a few feet in front of me so I could keep an eye on him while I worked." He was far enough away to be safe but close enough so she could get to him if he woke up.

Brad faced Brenda about 20 feet in front of her on his ladder.

"I was confident we could do this job with God's help," said Brenda. "I prayed silently that everything would go well and that we'd be safe from any harm as we worked."

Brenda remembered glancing at her husband as he loosened another 4 x 4 x 8 board with his crowbar. "Suddenly, the beam broke loose," she said. "It tumbled down, heading straight toward baby Patrick's head! I was horrified and stunned, realizing our son could be killed just like that."

Brenda hurried down her ladder from high overhead, but every step seemed to be in slow motion. Could she possibly reach her child fast enough to save him?

"Instantly I said a prayer of protection, begging God to keep the board from striking my baby." She envisioned God's holy light and love surrounding Patrick as she scrambled down the remaining slats.

At that point, the little guy appeared wide-awake and in a flash, moved his head *slightly* to the left. The board shaved his right cheek, missing his head by a fraction of an inch, before crashing onto the cement floor with a violent thud.

Oblivious to Brad's reaction as he stood on his ladder, Brenda hovered over her child in shock and wonder at how God had just performed a miracle in front of her eyes. There was no way she could have saved her son. Only God could—and did!

"On wobbly knees and shaking legs, I gave the Lord my undivided, heartfelt thanks for saving my son," Brenda shared.

Recalling that incident today, she was in tears. "I feel like a heel for what happened, but Brad and I never imagined such a thing would occur. I thought I had placed Patrick out of harm's way. This incident reaffirmed in me the importance of going beyond my human understanding. Nothing is impossible with our God. I thank him for all his forgiveness, mercy, and love."

Keep your fears to yourself, but share your courage with others.

Robert Louis Stevenson

Life-Changing Decision

We are hard pressed on every side, but not crushed;
perplexed, but not in despair.
2 CORINTHIANS 4:8

Joseph was engaged to the love of his life. He must have been ecstatic at the thought of taking the beautiful young Mary as his bride, building a life together, and, hopefully, raising a family. Soon they would exchange vows, and then they'd be alone—away from the whispers and nods and advice of the elders in the village. Everything was looking up. He even had a respectable trade as a carpenter and mason that would allow him to provide for his new wife and the children that would surely follow.

Then news he scarcely could imagine rocked his world. His lovely Mary was pregnant! How could that be? They hadn't been together. And surely Mary would not be with another man…

Joseph must have wrestled with God through prayer over this grave situation, tossing and turning at night, wondering how to respond to such an agonizing betrayal. He loved this woman!

When Mary said the Holy Spirit had come upon her and that she was to carry the Light of the World—Jesus, the Son of the most high God—Joseph was incredulous. What a story! He knew for certain the child wasn't his. Was Mary making up these details to save face? Infidelity carried a serious social stigma back in those days. Joseph not only had the right to back out of his commitment to marry Mary, but under Jewish law she could even be stoned to death.

Joseph's initial reaction was to break the engagement, the most appropriate thing for a righteous man to do. But, instead, he treated his beloved with great kindness. The last thing he wanted was for her to be shamed in front of the townspeople or, worse, lose her life. What should he do?

God met with Joseph in the nick of time, right where the young man was. God sent an angel to him in a dream to affirm Mary's story and reassure Joseph that his marriage to Mary was God's will. The angel explained that the Holy Spirit had helped Mary conceive the child, his name would be Jesus, and that he was the Messiah, "God with us," the one who would save the world.

When Joseph awakened from his dream, he obeyed God and took Mary home to be his wife, despite the public humiliation he would probably face. He was a good, faithful, and gentle man. Perhaps that was why God chose him to be Christ's earthly father.

How humbled and honored Joseph must have felt when he recalled the prophecy found in the book of Isaiah: "The Lord himself will give you a sign: The virgin will conceive and give birth to a son, and will call him Immanuel" (7:14).

Months later, Caesar Augustus decreed that a census be taken. Every person in the entire Roman world had to go to his hometown to register. Joseph, who was from the house and line of David, was required to go to Bethlehem. What an arduous journey he and Mary endured. Mary must have been physically uncomfortable since she was close to delivering her baby. According to James F. Strange, a New Testament and biblical archeology professor, their journey probably occurred in the winter when the daytime temperatures were in the 30s, nighttime temperatures in the freezing range, and rains were frequent. And when the couple arrived in Jerusalem, they discovered lodging was hard to come by.

When there was no room in any of the inns, Joseph had to take his young wife to a stable. While staying there, the child was born. "How could things get any worse?" Joseph may have thought. Yet God was with them! He provided the small manger to hold the babe, sent angels on high to praise the newborn king, and offered a bright star to guide the shepherds and wise men to the Christ child.

Joseph would face many more challenges as his young family

grew, but he remained faithful to God, to his wife, and to his children, becoming a positive example for followers of Jesus to honor and admire.

God places the heaviest burden on those who can carry its weight.
Reggie White

Ice Cream, Please

Be devoted to one another in love.
Honor one another above yourselves.
ROMANS 12:10

"It's so hard watching our parents age," my friend Kris said one day over coffee. Both of our mothers were victims of Alzheimer's disease. These dear, frail, old ladies who once carted us off to swimming lessons, led our Girl Scout meetings, taught us to knit and cook, now needed round-the-clock care. They barely recognized us as their daughters.

My mother was in a special facility, confined to a wheelchair during the day so she wouldn't fall and hurt herself or someone else. Kris's mom lived with her husband, who had become her caretaker. He too needed some looking after, and that fell to Kris, their only child. Without a sibling to share the responsibility, some days were just too much, especially after returning home from a full-time job. Kris's parents lived nearby so she was on-call to cook for them a few nights a week, to run errands, and to check on them each day.

"When Mom and Dad come for dinner, it's always difficult," Kris confessed. "It's hard to work all day and then cook—even for 'family company.'" Then Kris smiled as she told me about two wonderful things that had occurred the week before, taking her by complete surprise.

"My husband began pitching in on the nights when Mom and Dad were with us," she said. "Ron served, did the dishes, and helped my parents to and from the table. In fact, when Mom was at her worst, Ron seemed to be at his best! His caring ways and gentle words helped me calm down and see what God was doing through him."

One night when Kris's mother was having a particularly bad time, Kris watched as her husband reached over and patted her mother's hand. "She was crying, complaining, and very upset, a real trial to be around," said Kris. "But Ron knew just what to say. He didn't talk her out of crying or try to make her understand that she was disturbing everyone. No, he said simply, 'Mom, let's have some ice cream.' He knew it was her favorite dessert, and Mom's face lit up.

"What a change!" said Kris. "Mom seemed to forget her complaints and was, instead, ready to receive the treat Ron offered."

But it wasn't only Kris's mother who changed that night. Kris did as well. "In that moment, I saw my husband in a new light. I knew then that he would always treat me with the same love and care he extended to my mother, no matter what might happen to me in later life."

Kris was truly surprised at the feeling of joy and relief that came over her. And apparently it rippled throughout the room because minutes later her mother got up from the table, walked over to her own husband, and gave him a loving hug.

"I wish you could have seen my father's reaction," she added. "This simple gesture took him by complete surprise too. The depth of his appreciation was written all over his face." And all because God spoke to Ron, and Ron followed his lead by offering ice cream to his mother-in-law at the perfect time.

It is the spirit in a person, the breath of the Almighty,
that gives them understanding.

Job 32:8

Home Sweet Home

*Everyone who hears these words of mine and puts them into
practice is like a wise man who built his house on the rock.*
MATTHEW 7:24

Gloria and her son had lived in a rental house in Pico Rivera,
California, for six years. They were settled and happy there until
one morning the landlord phoned and informed Gloria he was putting the house on the market the next day. He wanted a quick sale
as soon as possible.

"After promising me over the years that he'd never sell, I was
taken by complete surprise," Gloria confessed. "I felt like the rug
had been pulled out from under me. I was a single mother with a
young child. I had no one to rely on to give me good advice or help
me make tough decisions. If the house sold, we'd have no choice but
to move—but to where? I had no idea."

For days Gloria wondered what to do. Then she felt God nudg-
ing her to trust him for the answer. She prayed for guidance every
day. "I kept reminding him about my dire financial situation and
the coming move. Weeks passed without a buyer for the house.
Then one night while I was praying, God whispered in my ear, 'Why
don't *you* buy it?'"

Gloria said she nearly laughed out loud. "I didn't know the first
thing about buying a house. And, even more important, I had absolutely no extra money. But I listened to that still small voice and
obeyed God every time I felt Him telling me what to do next." With

a little faith in herself and a lot more faith in God, she started the proceedings to purchase the house. "I'd always considered myself a strong person," said Gloria, "but now I felt afraid and vulnerable… even frantic. I couldn't imagine handling all the details on my own. I had a hard time concentrating at work as doubt crept in at every opportunity."

Gloria envisioned her and her son forced to live on the street. "At times it was difficult to pray without letting negative thoughts creep in. But I kept telling myself to trust the Lord. He would provide for us." She also read encouraging Scriptures. "One that I still rely on to this day is Jeremiah 32:27: 'I am the LORD, the God of all mankind. Is anything too hard for me?'"

According to Gloria, it was a challenge to let go of doubt, to stop depending on herself, and to leave everything in God's hands. "But I knew that trust and doubt don't mix. I reminded myself of Paul's words to the Philippians: 'My God will meet all your needs according to the riches of his glory in Christ Jesus'" (4:19).

At the close of escrow, the final cost of $1050 was due at the bank. "I had $2 in my purse! I got on my knees early that morning and released the whole situation to God. His presence was so overpowering that all my anxieties washed away. I had total peace. What a humbling experience!" She knew then that no matter what happened, God would take care of her son and her.

"The mailman came earlier than usual that morning, and he brought an envelope with a check I'd been waiting on for a month. Next, my neighbor knocked on my door and said the Lord had impressed on her to loan me $500. Then I remembered I had a small amount of money in my savings account. By the time I reached the bank for my afternoon appointment, I had $77 more than I needed!"

Gloria was in such a state of gratitude and praise that she couldn't help but share her miracle with the bank tellers and even the customers in line. Each one seemed eager to hear her story.

"Now, many years later, my son has long since grown and moved on with his life. I'm still enjoying my home in Pico Rivera. God is good. I talk to him constantly throughout the day," Gloria said. "I often whisper praises while sitting at my desk at work or even when walking through the parking lot. I know he is my true husband and friend, and I can depend on him to meet all my needs. At times the wait is longer than I would like it to be, but I just keep praying and expecting his answer. I also think back to that experience concerning my house and realize how powerful my God is. And I remember that I can do all things through Christ who strengthens me, as promised in Philippians 4:13. And he can and will do all things for me in his perfect timing."

Great opportunities to help others seldom come,
but small ones surround us every day.

Sally Koch

Heavenly Scholarship

The beginning of wisdom is this: Get wisdom.
Though it cost all you have, get understanding.
PROVERBS 4:7

During Kimberly Johnson's senior year in high school, she felt a strong and sudden urge to attend a college she'd never considered before. Based on her high score in a singing competition, she received word from the school that she'd be eligible to participate in auditions for music scholarships for prospective freshmen.

"The pressure was on big time," said Kimberly, "because my dad didn't want me to go away from home for college. I didn't have any savings of my own either, since I hadn't been allowed to work."

Finally, Kimberly's father agreed she could go, but only if she received a music scholarship. "I *had* to get it, and I believed with all my heart I would. My mother drove me to Kirkland, Washington, for the piano audition. I failed, leaving me stunned and in tears."

Kimberly wondered how she could feel so clearly that this was what God had for her and yet experience such a hopeless result. To sort out her thoughts and feelings, she walked outside the building and "found a quiet place on a wood bridge and cried my heart out to the Lord."

While praying, she felt God's peace wash over her. "I'd never experienced it so intensely before. In that moment I was confident I would attend Northwest in the fall."

That night, Kimberly and her mother attended a Mariners game and had a wonderful time. "My mom was baffled by my change in attitude. The last she'd seen me I was devastated. I told her that God had assured me I was going to attend this school."

The following morning in the campus chapel, all the students who had auditioned were seated, waiting for the scholarship winners to be announced. "I guess I thought God would turn my audition the day before into a scholarship-winning one, but to my shock, my name wasn't called." What is going on? Kimberly thought. She was certain God had spoken to her. "Again I was devastated and cried out to God. Had I missed something? He knew I couldn't go to school without that scholarship." She called her dad, and he was pleased she hadn't received the scholarship because he didn't want her to leave home yet. He'd even refused to allow Kimberly to accept her grandmother's offer to help with the tuition at Northwest.

Kimberly was totally confused. "I talked to God most of that four-hour drive home. Still bewildered at the turn of events, I walked in the front door to a ringing telephone. I answered it, and it was a representative from Northwest calling to offer me a scholarship. The person it was meant for couldn't accept it for some reason, and I was next in line."

God answered Kimberly's prayer in the nick of time. "He showed me that *he* awarded that scholarship, not the school. To this day I know that when God promises something, he will deliver. I can trust him even when things appear impossible."

Kimberly went on to graduate with a degree in behavioral science and a minor in music. She also met and married her husband while attending Northwest.

A moment's insight is sometimes worth a life's experience.
Oliver Wendell Holmes

Hard Call

*Oh, that their hearts would be inclined to fear me and keep
all my commands always, so that it might
go well with them and their children forever!*
DEUTERONOMY 5:29

Abraham loved the Lord with all his heart and soul. He followed God's commands even when he didn't understand them. Because of his loyalty, God promised to bless him greatly—and he did, providing cattle, silver, gold, and giving him the land of Canaan for his family and descendants.

In addition to all these riches, God blessed Abraham and his wife, Sarah, in their old age with a son whom they named Isaac. They loved this boy greatly.

Then God tested the faith of his servant Abraham. One day Abraham was told to take Isaac on a journey into the region of Moriah. When they arrived, Abraham was to build an altar and offer a sacrifice to God. This sacrifice would not be a ram or goat, as was the custom, but instead it was to be his beloved son Isaac.

What a strange and terrible command, Abraham must have thought. This didn't sound like the God he knew. But Abraham was certain God would never ask him to do something wrong, so he held on to his belief that even if he killed his son, God would raise him to life again (Hebrews 11:17).

The Bible doesn't say whether Abraham prayed for wisdom, but I figure that he did, especially since the request was unlike any God had made of him before. He may have knelt by his pallet at night and asked for an explanation or perhaps by day in the fields as he worked and prayed, wanting to be sure he'd heard God correctly. Probably even as he prepared for the journey he continued to ask for guidance.

On the day God had appointed, Abraham rose early in the morning, loaded his donkey, took along two of his servants, fire, a knife, and wood. The small party of travelers, along with Isaac, started on their journey. It took about three days for the group to arrive near the place God had indicated. Abraham left his men and most of the supplies at that point. He carried the knife and fire, while Isaac handled the firewood. They trudged up the mountain.

What a burden this father must have felt at the thought of sacrificing his young son.

> As the two of them went on together, Isaac spoke up and said to his father Abraham, "Father?"
>
> "Yes, my son?" Abraham replied.
>
> "The fire and wood are here," Isaac said, "but where is the lamb for the burnt offering?"
>
> Abraham answered, "God himself will provide the lamb for the burnt offering, my son." And the two of them went on together.
>
> When they reached the place God had told him about, Abraham built an altar there and arranged the wood on it. He bound his son Isaac and laid him on the altar, on top of the wood. Then he reached out his hand and took the knife to slay his son. But the angel of the LORD called out to him from heaven, "Abraham! Abraham!"
>
> "Here I am," he replied.
>
> "Do not lay a hand on the boy," he said. "Do not do anything to him. Now I know that you fear God, because you have not withheld from me your son, your only son" (Genesis 22:6-12).

In the nick of time God came through—answering the desire

of Abraham's heart that no harm would come to his son. Abraham then looked up and saw a ram caught in a thicket by its horns. He took the animal and offered it as a sacrifice to God.

The angel of the Lord called again to Abraham from heaven:

> Because you have done this and have not withheld your son, your only son, I will surely bless you and make your descendants as numerous as the stars in the sky and as the sand on the seashore. Your descendants will take possession of the cities of their enemies, and through your offspring all nations on earth will be blessed, because you have obeyed me (Genesis 22:15-18).

God had gone far beyond what Abraham could have imagined or wanted or prayed for. This was the God Abraham served, loved, and obeyed. He and Isaac returned to the servants, and the group set off for Beersheba, where Abraham lived.

It is for each of us freely to choose whom we shall serve,
and find in that obedience our freedom.
Mary Richards

Instead of striving to make this or that happen, we learn trust in a heavenly Father who loves to give. This does not promote inactivity, it does promote dependent activity. No longer do we take things into our own hands. Rather, we place all things into divine hands and then act out of inner promptings.

Richard J. Foster,
Prayer: Finding the Heart's True Home

Leader in Training

I will instruct you and teach you in the way you should go;
I will counsel you with my loving eye on you.
PSALM 32:8

Renetta's pastor approached her on several occasions with opportunities to use her leadership ability. During a recent mission trip, he asked her to stand and pray over a group of people. While on a tour bus he handed her the microphone, urging her to offer insights about a given topic and then lead a discussion with the passengers.

"Each time I declined," said Renetta, "even though I also felt the Lord's promptings to stand and speak and take the reins." She did her best to ignore God and her pastor because she didn't see herself as a leader. "I apologized to God for my failure, and then handed him my excuse, weak as it was: How can I lead when I'm not a leader? Yes, I'd graduated from college with a theology degree, but I hadn't attended seminary. I wasn't ordained, nor had I obtained any advanced training in the field of leadership." However, Renetta couldn't rest so she decided to pray about it.

"Kneeling at a makeshift altar in a small hospital chapel, I asked for God's guidance to help me discern whether this burden of leadership stemmed from my own thinking or a desire from the Holy Spirit. I'm one of those people who pray diligently throughout the day," she said. "The moment a thought or idea lands in my mind, I hold it up in prayer. I'm sure the Lord grew tired of my repeating the same concern, but I kept at it."

After the stirring she felt while on the mission trip, she became truly open and sensitive to any signs from God. "It could come through nature, a bird, an animal, or even an insect that crossed my path," said Renetta. "Perhaps the message would come from a friend, a neighbor, or a stranger on the street. Although I was hopeful, always on the lookout, I also felt agitated and nervous. My stomach was tied in knots, and I wept easily. What if the Lord actually answered my prayer? What if I turned out to be a terrible leader? What if people wouldn't follow? What if...? What if...?" These thoughts drove her night and day. "I was consumed with doubt."

After a series of "coincidences," Renetta applied to a Master's of Leadership Studies program. Applying didn't guarantee entrance. The new term was to start less than two weeks from the day she completed her application. "If I'd delayed any longer, my chances of acceptance would be slim to none. Within three days of my pursuit, I'd spoken to the dean of the college, delivered copies of my transcripts to the registrar's office, and submitted a paper I'd written for a freelance project months before."

The busy director of the leadership program was leaving for vacation that very afternoon so Renetta had no time to spare. "He agreed to interview me. Afterward, he gave me his stamp of approval."

Each of these steps had to take place before Renetta could be certain of her acceptance. "In the nick of time, I qualified and registered for the program. Talk about God's impeccable timing—this was it! I was in. Scared and ecstatic, I was on my way to becoming a credible leader."

Renetta said she learned so much about God's faithfulness and his timing during this process. "When prayers are offered up to him, if they are within his will, they'll be answered. And God will customize his response according to each of our needs. Our God is not only our guide and counselor, but also our loving father. He humbled me and renewed my sense of awe."

Renetta says she trusts more now, still consults the Lord on everything, even the simplest of details. "'Father, what do you think?' I ask. Believe it or not, I get a few simple words in my heart or sometimes a resounding 'yes' or 'no.' Then I know without a doubt which way to go.

"Now that I have my master's degree in leadership, I look with different lenses at those who carry the burden of leading others. The pursuit of being a good leader isn't about perfection or power or control. It's about service and humility. I also realized it's not necessary to have a degree. Everyone is a leader where they stand. The Lord gives each of us a sphere of influence. He leads, and then we follow and take on the leadership he calls us to."

Renetta is more comfortable now with God, with herself, and with her call to lead. She trusts the Lord to set the standard and determine her path in every situation.

No matter how many goals you have achieved,
you must set your sights on a higher one.
Jessica Savitch

Best Dress

I will bless her with abundant provisions.
PSALM 132:15

Kathryn and her husband had hit bottom. They were so desperate. Even the money they'd put aside for an emergency was nearly gone. Ted needed a job—and fast. He'd lost his position at a startup company when the investors pulled out. Kathryn needed some decent clothes if she were to go on an interview for a teaching position in the city where they'd settled just two months before.

They joined a church and started attending Sunday services, hoping to make new friends, to contribute their talents, and to find contacts for employment.

"I was an emotional wreck," Kathryn admitted. "I had prayed until words ran out. I didn't have the faith to continue. I believed that if God heard me, he'd have shown some mercy by that point. We'd be moving to the city shelter if something didn't turn up by the end of the month when our meager rent was due."

The first Sunday they walked into the church, a woman named Belinda approached them after the service and invited them to join a fellowship group held in her home. "We agreed to give it a try," said Ted. "If we couldn't pray for ourselves, maybe the group could pray for us."

Kathryn and Ted arrived at Belinda's house the following Tuesday night and felt right at home. Belinda and her husband, Bill, and two other couples welcomed them with warm words and loving prayers, asking God to pour his blessing into their lives in "good measure, pressed down, shaken together and running over" (Luke 6:38).

"We went home more hopeful than ever," said Kathryn. "The following week Bill stopped by with checks for $100 from each of the couples. That $300 made the difference between paying our rent and falling short. We would be okay for another month." Then came the startling and sad news that Belinda's mother passed away that same week from a long bout with cancer. "We wanted to do something for her, but what?" Ted said. "Kathryn decided to offer childcare so Belinda could meet with her siblings to make the final arrangements for her mother's burial."

Two weeks later, almost to the day, Belinda showed up at Kathryn and Ted's apartment carrying a large box. The couple invited her in. She sat down and opened the container. It was filled with dresses, a suit, several sweaters and blouses, and a jacket. "These belonged to Mom," she said, her eyes brimming with tears. "It would mean the world to me, Kathryn, if you'd wear them. You're about the same size she was, and many of these items are still in very good condition."

Kathryn's eyes filled with tears. This was just what she needed—enough clothing to see her through another season, and one of the dresses in particular would be ideal to wear to job interviews. She hurried into the bedroom and changed into one of the outfits. It fit perfectly! Belinda was thrilled, and Kathryn could hardly speak because of her gratitude.

God had not only answered her specific prayers, but he'd answered those of the home group too. And, as is often the case, he did so in the nick of time. He used each woman in the life of the other to bless both of them.

Within the year, Kathryn found a teaching job and Ted was invited to join a real estate firm.

If you want to make your dreams come true,
the first thing you have to do is wake up.
J.M. Power

Black Tuesday

Those who suffer he delivers in their suffering;
he speaks to them in their affliction.
JOB 36:15

My father-in-law, Charlie, loved to tell the story of how a friend came to his rescue on Black Tuesday back in 1929. Charlie had planned to withdraw some cash from his bank account the day before, but he got busy doing chores. He didn't make it before closing time. "I'll go first thing in the morning," he told his wife. But the next day was too late. The stock market had crashed. Banks closed for "reorganization," and many customers lost all but a few cents on the dollar.

Later that day, Charlie, consumed with worry and praying to God for guidance, met his friend Miles in the street and told him what had happened. On the spot, Miles reached into his pants pocket and pulled out $700 in cash. "It's all I've got in the world," he said. "But you've got nothing, Charlie. Here, half is yours!" He peeled off $350. "Pay me back when you can."

And Charlie did...with more than money. When Miles was confined to a bed during his last year of life, Charlie visited him every day. He fed him, prayed for him, and was an all-around good friend. But the story doesn't stop there.

Some 60 years later, a Ms. Butler stepped up to the customer service counter at a Nordstrom Department Store in La Jolla, California, to pay her bill. My husband, whose name was also Charles, worked there at the time. He commented on her last name. "Butler. I haven't heard that name in years. Miles Butler was my dad's best friend in Kentucky." Charles continued making small talk as he processed the woman's paperwork. Ms. Butler appeared interested, so Charles proceeded to tell her the story of his dad, Charlie, and his friend, Miles, on that fateful day when Miles had been such a good friend and shared half of all he had.

Two days later, Ms. Butler returned to the store with a message for my husband who was off that day. When Charles read the note the next day, he phoned me on the spot. "Listen to this!" he said, knowing I'd be interested in the follow-up to the incident with Ms. Butler.

"James Miles Butler was my paternal grandfather's brother," the note read. "My family and I thank you for what you shared. Until now we had no knowledge of this incident. Now we know what an exceptional human being Great-Uncle Miles was."

A moment of spontaneous generosity between two men who were now long gone gave birth to another moment of joy between two of their family members, who had an unplanned meeting decades later.

Only God can answer prayers across the generations, arranging a unique time for two people—and their families—to share a special moment.

If you cannot do great things, do small things in a great way.
Napoleon Hill

Woman of Courage

Wait for the LORD;
be strong and take heart and wait for the LORD.
PSALM 27:14

Sometime during the Bronze Age, between 2000 and 1550 BC, an Egyptian girl named Hagar became a slave to Sarai, a Hebrew princess and the wife of Abram. At the time it was a common practice to include slaves and servants as part of a marriage dowry. Hagar may have been part of the "bride price" Abram received from the pharaoh in Egypt. If Hagar was a gift from Pharaoh, she was probably an accomplished young woman with many useful skills. She may even have considered it a step down to join the household of a nomadic tribesman after living in a culture known for its temples, sophisticated economic system, and religious rites. Despite her skills and her former life, however, Hagar was nothing more than a foreigner and a slave in the eyes of the Hebrew women. But she became important to Abram and his wife when they were unable to conceive a child. In those times, bearing children was the primary role of a tribal leader's wife.

Sarai lived in constant grief over her barren state. She wondered why God wouldn't bless her with her a child, especially when he had promised to do so. And she couldn't tolerate being looked on as a failure in the eyes of her people. To resolve her shameful situation, she decided to take the matter into her own hands. She offered Hagar to Abram. Sarai had it all worked out. The young slave would

WHEN GOD ANSWERS YOUR PRAYERS

bear Abram's child and take care of it, but the baby would *belong* to Sarai and Abram and be treated as their own.

The Bible doesn't state whether anyone asked Hagar what she thought of this plan. But according to the customs of the day, it would have been an honor to become pregnant by the leader of the clan. So Hagar may have welcomed this opportunity to improve her social status.

So Abram "slept with Hagar, and she conceived. When she knew she was pregnant, she began to despise her mistress" (Genesis 16:4). What Sarai had thought was the perfect solution turned against her. Every day when the women interacted, Sarai was confronted by Hagar's ability to conceive a child and the young woman's disrespect toward her. Hagar, on the other hand, might have felt important for the first time in her life and enjoyed the positive attention she was receiving despite the effect it had on her mistress. This behavior infuriated Sarai to the point that she blamed her husband for what occurred, even though it had been her idea. "You are responsible for the wrong I am suffering. I put my slave in your arms, and now that she knows she is pregnant, she despises me. May the LORD judge between you and me."

Abram didn't take the bait! He said, "Your slave is in your hands... Do with her whatever you think best."

Sarai did just that. She humiliated Hagar and treated her harshly. The young woman ran off, heading south in a desperate attempt to return to her lost home and family in Egypt. She followed the road to Shur, one of the trade routes passing through the Sinai Peninsula. Alone and probably terrified, she persevered through the fearsome country with its unyielding wind and arid landscape. Surely Hagar must have prayed daily for help and comfort. Eventually, exhausted and overcome, she stopped. And God came through in the nick of time.

> The angel of the LORD found Hagar near a spring in the desert; it was the spring that is beside the road to Shur. And he said, "Hagar, slave of Sarai, where have you come from, and where are you going?"
>
> "I'm running away from my mistress Sarai," she answered.

Then the angel of the LORD told her, "Go back to your mistress and submit to her." The angel added, "I will increase your descendants so much that they will be too numerous to count."

The angel of the LORD also said to her:

"You are now pregnant and you will give birth to a son.

You shall name him Ishmael, for the LORD has heard of your misery.

He will be a wild donkey of a man; his hand will be against everyone and everyone's hand against him,
and he will live in hostility toward all his brothers."

Hagar listened to the angel of the Lord and returned to the tribe and to Sarai. I wonder what it was like for her to resume her role as a slave after being treated so poorly? The Bible doesn't say, but likely through prayer and God's mercy when she was at her lowest, Hagar realized she now had a high purpose for her life despite what others thought or said. She would bear a child who someday would have descendants without number.

When the time came, Hagar gave birth to her son, Ishmael. Fourteen years later, Sarai gave birth to Isaac. Ishmael was Abram's son and heir, confirming Hagar's noble status in the tribe and giving her a place of esteem in the Bible as a woman of courage and endurance.

The best way out is always through.
Robert Frost

Amazing Healing

*Heal me, LORD, and I will be healed; save me and
I will be saved, for you are the one I praise.*
JEREMIAH 17:14

"Twenty-four years ago I was diagnosed with Limb Girdle Muscular Dystrophy, a genetic, degenerative disease with no known cure or treatment," Beverly Adler shared. "I was teetering on the edge of losing major function. In recent years I could hardly use my left arm because it had become so weak. Atrophy had progressed to where my shoulder muscles were strained just to hold my arm in place."

Bev could hardly get out of a chair or stand up after bending over. "When possible, I tried not to shop, cook, or drive. In fact, I'd just received a referral for an adaptive driving assessment." This allows a driver with a disability to continue operating a vehicle that has been modified for his or her specific needs.

"Then I heard about MRS 2000, a 'Pulsed Electro Magnetic Field' (PEMF) technology. It's an incredible health system that fully maximizes every cell in your body while you lie for eight minutes on a full-body mat. There are also pillow-sized pads and a probe for specific areas that need restoration at a higher intensity." Bev said she didn't expect to notice any immediate benefit, but she was in for a real surprise when after three treatments (24 minutes) on the mat she felt stronger and walked much better than before. "I couldn't believe it!" she exclaimed. "I had to get this technology for myself and see what it could do for me."

After three weeks of using the MRS 2000, all of her functions improved. "My physical therapist could see in just a few days the difference in my range of motion and the substance of my muscle tissue. I was back to what was for me, in previous years, *normal* function." This technology was an answer to prayer and came in the nick of time. It has improved her resistance to an incurable, degenerative disease and increased for the better every aspect of Bev's health. "By changing the underlying cellular conditions (energizing, oxygenating, and alkalizing), I won't be vulnerable to a recurrence of the breast cancer I experienced two years ago. There is no price you can put on hope and peace of mind!"

Bev's entire family is experiencing surprising results. Her husband, Kai, feels 15 years younger. Both her parents, as well, have noticed chronic aging problems disappear. And a neighbor, who suffered from mononucleosis, used the system four times in two days and said, as she left for a vacation, "I haven't felt better in months." She returned reporting no setbacks.

"As I share the MRS 2000 with others," said Bev, "I am amazed at the various results people experience. There are dramatic published testimonials of canceled amputations, cancer tumors dissipated, and fibromyalgia and chronic fatigue overcome, to name just a few. This answer to prayers for my health over the years has been a life-changing discovery and hope-giving miracle for me. I wish for everyone with a medical challenge the same exciting experience of restored health and well-being that I've been privileged to enjoy—thanks to God who provides for each of us as we pray."

Patience is the companion of wisdom.
Saint Augustine

So Long, Dallas

Never be lacking in zeal,
but keep your spiritual fervor,
serving the Lord.
ROMANS 12:11

"In June 1976, my wife and I needed to sell the house in Dallas, Texas, that we'd owned during my years in seminary," said Pastor Jon Drury. "The time for our move to Washington State and the beginning of our new ministry there were right around the corner." After four years of constant study and class schedules, the couple rejoiced in a beautiful graduation ceremony and the life that lay ahead.

Jon recalled the many nights when he "wrote a paper till one o'clock in the morning while Bev slept. Then she would get up and type till dawn. As our kids awoke, I ripped my assignment out of the typewriter and ran out the door."

They prepared their house for sale, and prospective buyers began looking, but no one made an offer. The night before they were to leave Texas, everything necessary for their move was in place except the sale of their house. "Why didn't we get even a single offer?" Jon wondered aloud. "Have we done something wrong?" It appeared they'd drive off, uncertain of what was to become of the empty house. The family was physically ready to go, their furniture and belongings carefully packed and loaded onto the moving van. But their emotions waffled between nostalgia and fear.

"The time in seminary had been demanding in the extreme," Jon said. "But our house, built in old East Dallas in the 1920s, had been a refuge for us. It was surrounded by native pecan trees, summer fireflies, and friendly neighbors. We also attended a nearby church where we'd made good friends and had priceless opportunities to serve the community."

Their departure for the new pastorate couldn't be delayed. Their journey north would include a few stops—a visit to Jon's home church in the San Francisco Bay area for his ordination ceremony and a weekend in Colorado for a conference. Days later they would finally pull up in front of their new home and then explore the 80-member rural Baptist church where Jon would be the new pastor.

"We felt confident this was God's direction for our lives," Jon said. "But if so, where was the buyer we needed?"

The couple had done everything they knew to bring about a sale. After they read Bible stories in the evening with their children, they all prayed their house would sell. "David, our brown-haired, enthusiastic four-year-old prayed with simple faith for the sale," said Jon. One-year-old Chandra was too young to pray, but her bubbly personality encouraged them. Still no change, so they took the next step. They packed up the small items needed for their journey into their copper-colored Ford Pinto that would carry the family north.

"The night before we were to leave, just as it was getting dark outside," said Jon, "we heard a knock on our door. We answered, and the woman standing there introduced herself as a single mom in need of a home for her family. We showed her the house. Then she walked to the front lawn and stood there, surveying the property. With excitement in her voice, she said, 'It's exactly what I've been looking for!'"

The ideal buyer, thanks to God, had shown up. "We could hardly believe it. I don't remember when such a huge request has been answered with so few hours to spare. It was like the pillar of cloud and fire for God's people in the wilderness. It was evidence that God was there controlling our every step and reminding us to rely on him through all our days."

What is the difference between an obstacle and an opportunity?
Our attitude toward it. Every opportunity has a difficulty, and
every difficulty has an opportunity.

J. Sidlow Baxter

If a "leading" is of God the way will always open for it. Our Lord assures us of this when He said in John 10:4, "And when he putteth forth his sheep, he goeth before them, and the sheep follow him: they know his voice." Notice here the expressions "goeth forth" and "follow." He goes before to open a way, and we are to follow in the way thus opened. It is never a sign of a divine leading when the Christian insists on opening his own way, and riding roughshod over all opposing things. If the Lord "goes before" us, He will open the door for us, and we shall not need to batter down doors for ourselves.

Hannah Whitall Smith,
The Christian's Secret of a Happy Life

Pretty in Pink

That person is like a tree planted by streams of water,
which yields its fruit in season.
PSALM 1:3

Jeannie admits she's a pauper at heart. "I never find work that pays enough to cover the basics, and when I do have a few extra dollars from a gift or working overtime, I can't hold on to them."

Sitting across the cafe table from me, she looked off to the side and smiled. Then she turned back and continued. "For most of my life I've had a hard time buying myself the clothes I need," she said. "I usually wear an old T-shirt to bed, but what I really *wanted* was a beautiful, pink nightgown."

Someone had once told her she looked pretty in pink and that had stuck with her.

Then one day as she and her husband were driving, Jeannie noticed some fabric lying by the side of the road. "We had to stop. It was pink! My husband pulled over, and I jumped out of the car. I ran back and picked it up. It was a pink nightie—embossed, stylish, and it appeared to be brand-new. It still had a store tag on it! 'Oh, dear God!' was all I could say. It felt like someone had knocked the breath out of me I was so amazed."

Jeannie hopped back into the car and thanked God. He'd answered a prayer she'd barely uttered. She'd wanted to break her cycle of believing she wasn't enough as a person…and that there would never be enough in the world for her. She'd always felt overlooked and deprived no matter what happened. But not this time!

"I told the Lord that very minute, however and wherever he brings things into my life, it's great with me, even if it's in the street," she said and laughed. "Knowing God is the most astounding thing that ever happened to me. I align my will with his and hear him gently telling me he will *always* provide what I need." She giggled. "And I think I hear him saying, 'You look pretty in pink!'"

All meaningful and lasting change starts first in your imagination
and then works its way out.

Albert Einstein

Beloved Brother

He remembers his covenant forever,
the promise he made, for a thousand generations.
PSALM 105:8

Mary and Martha of Bethany loved their brother, Lazarus, with full hearts, so when he suddenly fell ill they were very worried. There was only one thing to do: Get a message to their friend, Jesus. "Lord, the one you love is sick." When they didn't hear back for two days, they became further distressed. Why didn't he come? Had their message been lost or delayed? I imagine they began praying every hour, maybe even minute-by-minute, begging God to heal their beloved brother. Perhaps they took turns waiting by the window, watching and hoping Jesus would arrive any moment to restore Lazarus's health.

Meanwhile, Jesus said to his disciples when he received the message from Lazarus's sisters, "This sickness will not end in death. No, it is for God's glory so that God's Son may be glorified through it... Our friend Lazarus has fallen asleep; but I am going there to wake him up" (John 11:4,11).

The disciples, assuming he was talking about real sleep, like people do at the end of the day, reassured Jesus that Lazarus would get better as soon as he had enough rest. They didn't see any reason to make the journey to his house, especially since word was out that the Jewish leaders were plotting to kill Jesus. Then Jesus spoke to them plainly. "Lazarus is dead, and for your sake I am glad I was not there, so that you may believe. But let us go to him" (verses 14-15).

By the time they arrived, Lazarus had been buried in the tomb for four days. When Martha heard Jesus was near the village, she ran ahead to meet him, but her sister Mary stayed at home.

"Lord," Martha said to Jesus, "if you had been here, my brother would not have died." At that point she might have regretted her choice of words and her accusative tone. She backed down. "But I know that even now God will give you whatever you ask."

"Your brother will rise again," Jesus told her.

At first his words did little to comfort Martha. "I know he will rise again in the resurrection at the last day," she said. What she and Mary really wanted more than anything was for Lazarus to arise now—in their midst—and go home with them. She didn't want to wait until the end of time. But she was sure that was impossible.

Jesus must have smiled at her concern and maybe even laid a hand on her shoulder or comforted her with a brotherly embrace as he spoke these unforgettable words: "I am the resurrection and the life. The one who believes in me will live, even though they die; and whoever lives by believing in me will never die. Do you believe this?"

"Yes, Lord," Martha answered. "I believe that you are the Messiah, the Son of God, who is to come into the world."

Then she went home and called for her sister Mary. "The Teacher is here...and is asking for you." Mary got up and went to him. Friends who were at the house mourning followed Mary to where Jesus was. Mary fell at Jesus's feet and she too said, "Lord, if you had been here, my brother would not have died."

Jesus was so moved by her weeping and the mourning of her friends, that he wept with them. "Where have you laid him?" he asked. By then Martha had returned, and many of their friends were gathered around.

The sisters took Jesus to the tomb where Lazarus's body had been placed. The skeptics in the crowd whispered, "Could not he who opened the eyes of the blind man have kept this man from dying?" Jesus didn't bother to reply to their cutting remarks. He did what he knew his Father in heaven wanted.

"Take away the stone," Jesus said.

"But, Lord…by this time there is a bad odor, for he has been there four days." Once again, Martha appeared to be correcting her master, even though she'd said she believed in him.

"Did I not tell you that if you believe, you will see the glory of God?" Jesus asked.

Martha didn't understand his words, but she decided to do what he requested. Some men took away the stone covering the tomb's entrance. Then Jesus prayed. "Father, I thank you that you have heard me. I knew that you always hear me, but I said this for the benefit of the people standing here, that they may believe that you sent me." Then he called in a loud voice, "Lazarus, come out!"

And Lazarus came out just as Jesus commanded.

Although Martha and Mary thought Jesus was too late, he came in the nick of time to quiet the skeptics and reaffirm who he was to his followers. Jesus told the bystanders, "Take off [Lazarus's]…grave clothes and let him go" (John 11:44).

And so they did!

───⁓◌⁓───

Man is made by his belief. As he believes, so he is.
Johann Wolfgang von Goethe

Fifty Years

*I was young and now I am old, yet I have never seen the
righteous forsaken or their children begging bread.*
Psalm 37:25

Dorothy's preteen children got fed up fast with her zealous
behavior after she gave up drinking and became a follower of Christ.
"I was so relieved and happy to know Jesus," she said, "that I wanted
my kids and my husband to experience the same joy. But I went
about it all wrong. I realize that now." She'd dragged her son and
daughter off to "children's church" despite their protests, and she'd
begged her husband to join her for Sunday services. The kids didn't
have a choice since she was their mom, but her husband did. He
chose to stay home. And he continued to do so for the next 50 years.

After Addy and Wally grew up and moved out, they went their
own ways. Dorothy didn't see much of either one for many years.
She missed them, but as time went on she released them to the Lord.
She always prayed that someday they would come to know their
Lord and Savior. Her husband, Fred, was an alcoholic and gambler,
just as Dorothy had been, so family relationships were strained and
stress reigned when they all got together.

Fred liked Reno, Atlantic City, and Las Vegas. In fact, they were
the only cities he was interested in visiting. He wanted Dorothy to
continue to accompany him on these once-a-year trips, and she did
reluctantly.

"As a new Christian," she recalled, "I searched every page of the

Bible looking for a way out of my marriage, but I could never find one. Fred had not strayed with other women as far as I knew. In fact, he always wanted me around—to sit with him at night while he watched television, to take walks in the neighborhood together, and to fix his favorite steak dinners."

As he aged, Fred cut back on drinking because his body couldn't tolerate it anymore, but his cold temperament and lack of communication about anything meaningful continued. Dorothy admitted she felt alone in the marriage. But still she remained, devoting herself to prayer every morning.

She became a spiritual mother to many women, including me. I relied on her for wisdom, practical advice, and encouragement in my own marriage and family life. She always seemed to know just the right thing to say and would point me to the perfect Bible verse for the situation or day.

Years later, when Fred and Dorothy were in their eighties, Dorothy had a serious fall and Fred suffered a stroke. Their children moved them to a nursing home because they needed more care than the son and daughter could provide. Fred became so angry over this change in their lives that he wouldn't speak to Dorothy or his children. So he and Dorothy were placed in private rooms in separate wings of the facility. It was a horrible way to end their nearly 50 years of marriage.

Dorothy never gave up praying for her husband's salvation. More than anything in the world she wanted him to know Christ and be assured of his home in heaven, knowing they could be friends there.

One day Jean, a young woman from Dorothy's former church, came by to visit. She told Dorothy she'd stopped at Fred's room after hearing he was close to his last hour. He was breathing heavily, and his eyes were closed. His doctor expected him to slip into a coma before long. Jean took that opportunity to sit by his side and talk to him about Christ. She said he listened without saying a word, but tears slipped down his cheeks. "Fred," she asked, "do you know where you're going when all this is over?"

He just shook his head.

"Wouldn't you like to know?"

He nodded.

Jean took his hand and told him that Jesus was waiting for him. All he had to do was accept the invitation to make Jesus Lord of his life, and then he'd be assured of eternal life. And he'd see his beloved Dorothy in heaven when it was time for her to leave the earth. She shared what life outside of heaven might be like, then she went on to tell Fred that in the next life there would be no more tears, no more anger, and no more pain.

Fred squeezed her hand, and she led him in a prayer of repentance and submission. Within minutes of that event, he crossed over from life on earth to eternal life in heaven.

When Dorothy heard this news she broke down. God had answered her prayer just in time. She and Jean held hands and prayed, thanking God for his love and faithfulness.

The following year Dorothy followed Fred to heaven.

Patience and perseverance surmount every difficulty.

Anonymous

Second Chance

*If you forgive other people when they sin against you,
your heavenly Father will also forgive you.*
MATTHEW 6:14

Liz and Carla had been friends for 20 years when a storm of words blew their relationship apart. Each believed she was in the "right." Carla was the strong, bossy type. Liz was compliant until she was pushed too far. There seemed to be no way to heal the wounds to go backward or forward. Their friendship was over.

"Good riddance as far as I was concerned," Liz admitted. "Relief flooded my soul when I realized I wouldn't have to put up with Carla's opinions and declarations anymore. I did feel guilty for not parting on civil terms, but not guilty enough to do anything about it."

Liz said their family life was a mess for many months after the breakup because the children and husbands were affected. The kids had played together for years, and the husbands enjoyed competing against each other in tennis regularly. Time spent together with the Kenyons ceased. And opportunities to visit with Carla's wonderful parents were gone.

"I hoped and prayed God would intervene and wake up Carla to her mistakes," said Liz. "It didn't occur to me to pray for my own because it was so clear that she was to blame."

Life went on and the discomfort subsided over the following years. The women avoided each other whenever possible. "If I saw Carla at the supermarket, I'd move to a different aisle. If our paths crossed when hauling kids to and from school, we turned our eyes away from one another," Liz said.

Several years later Liz was divorced and lived in a new city. When Liz's eldest daughter, Jane, was planning her wedding, she asked if Carla and Bob could be included on the guest list. "My stomach turned at the thought," Liz admitted. "I didn't want this special day to be compromised. But for Jane's sake, I agreed. The couple's grown children would be invited too."

Liz prayed about the event, asking for peace and joy—or at least civility if nothing else when she came into contact with Carla. "God gave me so much more," said Liz, "and all in the nick of time."

As Carla came across the lawn in a beautiful spring dress, smiling broadly, Liz melted. "I rushed toward her with open arms, and she did the same toward me. I'm sure God raised my arms for me. We embraced as we never had before. I felt a genuine love for her—Christ's love, I'm sure.

"'I've missed you,' Carla said to me, and her words pierced my heart like a sword. I realized then that I'd missed her too. I told her so. We both wept and laughed and smiled and held hands as we walked over to visit in the shade of a tree in front of the church."

The two women let go of the past just like that. They talked only of good things—family, work, parents, and health. "Carla had aged," said Liz. "And of course I had too. I liked what I saw in her—a soft countenance, a gentler way of speaking, a willingness to hear about my life."

At the end of the day, the bride and groom left for their honeymoon and the guests departed. "As my husband and I drove home, I thanked God for his mercy and grace," Liz shared. "I didn't know what was ahead for Carla and me. We lived in different cities now, and things had changed a lot in our lives from the old days. But I felt set free and able to love without reservation or judgment. Maybe that was enough."

Forgiveness is a gift you give yourself.
Suzanne Somers

God's House

What shall we wear?
MATTHEW 6:31-32

By the beginning of the summer of 2011, Charlie, a Realtor, and his wife had used every bit of financial reserve they had to pay their outstanding bills. "We'd been trying to work out a modified home loan with our bank but weren't making any progress," Rhonda said. "We'd tapped into our retirement, but we couldn't continue to do so."

The couple started praying verses from the Bible, especially from the book of Isaiah. Isaiah 54:17 was a favorite: "No weapon forged against you will prevail." Rhonda said, "We stood on that verse and applied it to the weapons of famine, bankruptcy, and drought. We added to it Scriptures that promised harvest, blessing, and renewal."

They felt full of trust one day, but fearful the next when more bills arrived. "The more I read and believed," said Rhonda, "the more God stirred my faith. I knew I had to get to the place where I was willing to let go of our home and move if we had to. I began to release *all* of our concerns and worries to God."

Rhonda prayed over her husband, asking the Lord to give him favor with clients. "A new season of harvest started to unfold in the area of our finances." Before long, new realty customers showed up, made offers on homes for sale, and the offers were accepted. But then some fell through, and the couple got discouraged again. "I battled against the obstacles and pleaded the blood of Jesus over each one," Rhonda shared. "I asked God to give Charlie wisdom and the ability to find solutions so nothing would sabotage the sales in escrow."

At the end of the summer, he'd closed on two homes in the nick of time. "We were able to pay our monthly bills," said Rhonda with a big sigh. "We also took another important step. We repented to God for our previous poor stewardship with the money he'd provided. Although we'd paid our weekly tithe at church, we hadn't fulfilled our missions pledge because of our financial drought." They made up the shortfall, and asked God for guidance in handling future income. "We didn't realize we'd been burying our seed in rocky dirt instead of sowing it in healthy soil," she said. "Once we put our affairs in order, changes happened for the better."

Rhonda said she learned that with prayer comes obedience. "If we are stuck in a situation we can't figure out on our own, we ask God what is blocking his blessing. If it's something we're doing in disobedience, then we know we have to make it right in his eyes."

Now Rhonda and Charlie have faith for other challenges. This experience has also heightened their faith when praying for others. "I trust God more than ever to hear and answer my prayers for us and for our family and friends," Rhonda said. "We're still on a journey regarding our house finances. But until God moves us out, we're treating it like it's ours. I no longer dread leaving if we have to. In fact, we painted the kitchen and made a few improvements by faith. If it turns out that we lose our home, then we believe God has another plan for us. But in the meantime, this house is our home, and we are being good stewards."

It's not what you look at that matters, it's what you see.
Henry David Thoreau

A Promise Kept

You make me glad by your deeds, LORD;
I sing for joy at what your hands have done.
PSALM 92:4

Mary and Joseph arrived at the temple in Jerusalem to dedicate their infant son, Jesus, when he was 40 days old as was the custom. The couple had little money to spare, so they offered two turtledoves instead of the customary lamb as their sacrifice. Simeon, a holy man and noted scholar, greeted them with warmth and anticipation. He'd spent much time studying the teachings of the prophets of Israel. During his studies, he'd learned of the coming of the Messiah, who would deliver Israel from its conquerors. From that time on, Simeon had devoted many years to praying faithfully for the Messiah's birth. During one prayer session, the Holy Spirit revealed to him that he would not die before he'd seen the Messiah (Luke 2:26).

The Jewish people had looked forward to the Messiah's birth for thousands of years, and God graciously chose to bless Simeon by communicating directly with him. Clearly a man of great faith and hope, Simeon had prayed and waited for this moment nearly his entire adult life. Moved by the Spirit, he went to the temple courts. When Joseph and Mary arrived, Simeon took the baby Jesus into his arms and prophesied confidently. He said to Mary, "This child is destined to cause the falling and rising of many in Israel, and to be a sign that will be spoken against, so that the thoughts of many hearts will be revealed" (verses 34-35).

What an amazing sight it must have been for Simeon to gaze at this tiny babe whose life and death on the cross would bring salvation to the world and reconciliation with God. Likely in his eighties or older at the time he held the child, Simeon was then ready to die, for God had fulfilled his promise! The holy man praised God, saying, "Sovereign Lord, as you have promised, you may now dismiss your servant in peace. For my eyes have seen your salvation, which you have prepared in the sight of all nations: a light for revelation to the Gentiles, and the glory of your people Israel."

This brief entry in the Bible isn't long on details, but it does exemplify in clear language that God keeps his promises. He never fails. He rewards faithful prayers!

Faithfulness and truth are the most sacred excellences
and endowments of the human mind.
Marcus Tullius Cicero

"Be not anxious for the morrow." This is not to be taken as a philosophy of life or a moral law: it is the gospel of Jesus Christ, and only so can it be understood. Only those who follow him and know him can receive this word as a promise of the love of his Father and as a deliverance from the thralldom of material things. It is not care that frees the disciples from care, but their faith in Jesus Christ...It is senseless to pretend that we can make provision because we cannot alter the circumstances of this world. Only God can take care, for it is he who rules the world.

Dietrich Bonhoeffer,
The Cost of Discipleship

Close Call

The LORD is my rock, my fortress and my deliverer.
PSALM 18:2

Sam picked up his grandson from school and dropped him off at home. Then he took a quick side trip to the bank in town to deposit a couple of checks. "I walked out of the building and started toward my car when suddenly I noticed smoke billowing from underneath my car's frame. I unlocked the driver's door so I could pop open the hood. As soon as I did, flames shot out! I slammed the hood and jumped back."

People were gathering around the site, and one man handed Sam his phone to call the fire department. "Would you call for me?" he asked. "I'm too shook up."

Minutes later the firemen arrived and doused the flames. Later the car was hauled away as scrap metal.

"I let out a sigh of relief and a prayer of thanks," said Sam. "What a close call that had been! My grandson and I could have been in the car when the engine caught fire and exploded."

After the shock wore off, Sam faced a new challenge. He was without wheels. He'd need a replacement vehicle—a nice little truck, if available—for a price he could afford. And $5000 was his limit.

The next day he and his wife, Jan, looked at used cars and trucks in their community. "I have a feeling there's one out there for you," said Jan. "I just know it."

Sam voiced his surprise. "I doubt we can find something this soon. It's going to take a couple of weeks, and we'll probably have to visit several lots to be sure. Meanwhile I guess we'll have to share your car."

The couple took a long walk that day, praying for guidance, for a car salesperson they could trust and work with, and for the right deal at the right price at the right time. God had always answered their prayers for vehicles in the past, so they trusted him for this one too.

Not long after that, the twinkle in Jan's eye told Sam she was on to something. Knowing his wife as he did, they might land a car that very day. They pulled up to Ernie's Used Car Lot, and within minutes Jan spotted a clean white GM "Jimmy" with a truck base for $5600. Yep, it was $600 over their budget. "Hmm," Sam admitted. "I had second thoughts at that point. "Figuring that and the sales tax, the vehicle was well beyond what we could afford."

A salesman walked over and began touting the truck's wonderful features, which were plentiful for a 15-year-old vehicle. He explained how it had just come on the lot the day before, was previously owned by only one person, and had a mere 60,000 miles on it.

"At that point Jan took over," said Sam. "She inspected the car inside and out, and we took turns test driving it. Neither of us could believe what great shape it was in. I knew this was the little truck for me."

Jan, however, wasn't going to settle for the asking price. "We have $5000 cash available," she said. "Not a penny more. And that needs to include the sales tax and any other miscellaneous expenses. Can you work with us?"

"I'll speak with my manager," said the salesman. "I'll be right back."

When he returned, Sam had one additional stipulation. He wanted their son-in-law, Grant, who owns an auto repair shop, to inspect it. The manager agreed. The next day the report from Grant arrived. The truck needed a part that would cost $800.

"Whoa! That nearly broke the deal," Sam shared. "But God came in with an answer to our silent prayer in the nick of time. The manager said he'd have his technician replace the part without cost to us. And, furthermore, we could have the car for the five grand, including sales tax. That meant I'd have a new-to-me vehicle for $5000 out the door."

Two days later the couple drove the shiny white Jimmy off the lot. They've enjoyed it without encountering a problem for the past three years. "I see now that I can't put anything past God...or Jan! When those two get together through prayer, I can always expect the unexpected."

Vision is the art of seeing things invisible to others.
Jonathan Swift

Crossroads

*The generous will themselves be blessed,
for they share their food with the poor.*
PROVERBS 22:9

In the year 2000, Charise volunteered to be part of a weeklong missions trip to Costa Rica. "During that visit," she said, "one of the pastors told me he knew God was doing something big in my life. Little did I know that in less than a year I would land at a major crossroad. That's when the opportunity to return to Costa Rica and work without pay for a social service agency and missionary presented itself. So did the opportunity to go back to a job that I hated but paid very well and provided excellent benefits."

Charise mulled over both choices. She felt led to Costa Rica, but it didn't make any sense. "I was a single mother with a seven-year-old daughter. How could I consider a volunteer position in another country when I had a *real* job waiting for me here in the United States?" she shared.

Charise handed the obstacles to the Lord, trying to convince herself how impossible it was to make the move to Costa Rica. But God resolved every one of them. "I had a lease on an apartment. The leasing agent told me he'd waive the agreement so I wouldn't lose any money. I had nowhere to store my belongings, but a friend from church offered to keep my furniture at her property without cost to me. I had a car loan to consider. The bank rep said he'd defer my payments."

Despite all this help, Charise still wasn't convinced going to Costa Rica was the right thing to do. "To make sure, I sent an email to the agency's director to get her opinion. This was my final test to see if God was the one providing all these green lights. Weeks went by without a reply."

Then Charise began to fret in the opposite direction. She *wanted* to go to Costa Rica, but since she hadn't received a reply to the email she assumed the answer from God was no. "I had to make a final decision soon because the manager at the company that had offered me the paid job needed to know whether I was coming back. I spoke with a Christian friend about this dilemma on a Sunday afternoon. 'Pray about it till Friday,' she advised."

Charise prayed, apologizing to God for testing him like this. But she sincerely believed she needed a confirmation from the missions director before she could make a wise decision. "I specifically remember including in my prayer the words 'Friday or even before' and the phrase 'the sooner the better.'" She also prayed the Lord's Prayer "in case that one would do the trick." She continued. "I lay in bed, and then I slid out and got down on my knees. I prayed with my eyes open, my eyes closed, my hands folded, my hands 'steepled,' and my hands up in the air. I said prayers every way I had ever heard of to make sure I did it right." Because the idea of going to Costa Rica was so outside her comfort zone, Charise was in a perpetual state of anxiety. "I was trying to be rational and logical, but God kept putting things in my path that shook me to my core. Seven hours after I gave God a week to get back to me, the director, thrilled to hear I was seriously considering moving, *phoned* me from Costa Rica. That removed all doubt."

God had answered her prayer just in time. "I felt humbled and grateful that he loved me so much that he'd put up with my childish ways," Charise shared. Then a pastor reminded her of the story of Gideon, who asked God to give him a sign by causing a piece of wool that he set out overnight to be wet in the morning. Then he did it again except asking God to make it dry in the morning. "I decided Gideon and I would have gotten along," Charise shared with a smile.

"I learned in this instance that God can handle the big things and the little things. He is God in *all* things. I was praying for an email and received a phone call instead. And it changed my life and my daughter's life in profound ways."

One way to keep momentum going is to have constantly greater goals.
Michael Korda

From Bad to Good

God is our refuge and strength,
an ever-present help in trouble.
PSALM 46:1

It was to be a "bad news day" for Joe Phillips, insurance agent. He was eager to make a sale and earn the commission necessary to keep his family going. "I was dreading the coming meeting something fierce," he said. "My prospective clients, Wes and Betty, had each applied for $100,000 of life insurance. Wes was turned down, but Betty made it through the process. I feared that Wes would be so upset to learn the company wouldn't issue a policy on him that he'd refuse to buy one on his wife."

As Joe traveled east on Highway 198 toward Lindsay, California, to meet with his clients, his heart was pounding and his palms were perspiring. He petitioned God, as he had many times before, with a prayer motivated by panic and the desire for what *he* wanted when he wanted it. "Lord, please help me make this sale in spite of everything," he begged.

In that moment, Joe suddenly discerned he was not alone in the car. "*Someone* was actually listening to me," he reported later. "And that someone interrupted my prayer with these words. 'There you go again, praying selfishly.' I knew instantly it was the Lord, and his meaning was clear.

"I began praying from my heart. 'Lord, you're right. You are the alpha and the omega. You are the only one who knows if these folks are to acquire the policy or not. If it's right in your eyes, then please have it work out for Betty. And if it's not, then okay. Amen.'" Joe claims in that moment a spirit of peace came over him. As he drove to the appointment he sang the beautiful hymn "Holy God, We Praise Thy Name." He arrived on time, trusting God for the perfect answer according to *his* will. The Lord heard his heartfelt plea and answered. The couple purchased the policy on Betty without delay. Joe walked out the door with much more to be thankful for than one commission on a sale. He'd received a lesson in humility and prayer that he's never forgotten.

Opportunity dances with those who are already on the dance floor.

Jackson Brown

Wit and Wisdom

I will praise the LORD, who counsels me;
even at night my heart instructs me.
PSALM 16:7

David and his warriors were traveling in an area where Nabal was working with his servants taking care of his flocks. Upon hearing that the men were shearing sheep nearby, David sent 10 of his young men to see him.

> Go up to Nabal at Carmel and greet him in my name. Say to him: "Long life to you! Good health to you and your household! And good health to all that is yours! Now I hear that it is sheep-shearing time. When your shepherds were with us, we did not mistreat them, and the whole time they were at Carmel nothing of theirs was missing. Ask your own servants and they will tell you. Therefore be favorable toward my men, since we come at a festive time. Please give your servants and your son David whatever you can find for them" (1 Samuel 25:5-8).

Nabal, true to his nature, answered David's servants with caustic words:

> Who is this David? Who is this son of Jesse? Many servants are breaking away from their masters these days. Why should I take my bread and water, and the meat I have

slaughtered for my shearers, and give it to men coming
from who knows where? (verses 10-11).

When David's men returned, they reported Nabal's critical
response. This was hardly the answer David had wanted or expected.
It was the custom in those days to share food with a person's protec-
tors even if they didn't ask for it. David, the warrior, was determined
to retaliate. "Each of you strap on your sword!" he commanded.
Then he took 400 men and headed out to visit Nabal personally.

One of the servants, having witnessed the scene between Nabal
and David's men, ran to Nabal's wife, Abigail, to report what had
happened. She knew there was not a moment to waste. If she didn't
act fast, her entire household and community might be dead by
morning. She must have begun praying immediately. She also
trusted God to enable her to do what needed to be done. Quickly
she assembled 200 loaves of bread, 2 skins of wine, 5 sheep ready to
cook, some roasted grain, a supply of raisins, and 200 fig cakes. She
had it all loaded onto donkeys. Then she ordered her servants to go
before her to meet David. She said she would follow.

As she rode on a donkey over a hill and down the other side,
she saw David and his army coming toward her. Here was another
opportunity to pray, I'm sure! When she was near the king, Abigail
immediately slid down from her animal, fell on her face, and bowed
to the ground in front of him. Then she spoke up.

> Pardon your servant, my lord, and let me speak to you; hear
> what your servant has to say. Please pay no attention, my
> lord, to that wicked man Nabal. He is just like his name—
> his name means Fool, and folly goes with him. And as for
> me, your servant, I did not see the men my lord sent. And
> now, my lord, as surely as the LORD your God lives and as
> you live, since the LORD has kept you from bloodshed and
> from avenging yourself with your own hands, may your
> enemies and all who are intent on harming my lord be like
> Nabal. And let this gift, which your servant has brought to
> my lord, be given to the men who follow you.

"Praise be to the LORD, the God of Israel, who has sent you today to meet me," David replied. "May you be blessed for your good judgment and for keeping me from bloodshed this day and from avenging myself with my own hands. Otherwise, as surely as the LORD, the God of Israel, lives, who has kept me from harming you, if you had not come quickly to meet me, not one male belonging to Nabal would have been left alive by daybreak" (verses 32-34).

Abigail used her wit and wisdom, and by the grace of God averted tragedy for her household. The next day Abigail told Nabal all that had happened, and "his heart failed him and he became like a stone." Within two weeks he died. When David heard that Nabal was dead, the king thanked the Lord for intervening and for dealing with Nabal's wrongdoing. David was so impressed by Abigail's beauty, wisdom, and courage, that he sent his servants to see her and deliver his marriage proposal!

A good head and a good heart are always a formidable combination.
Nelson Mandela

Final Answer

Those who sow with tears will reap with songs of joy.
PSALM 126:5

"Get in and get out," I told myself. "This is no time for chitchat."
At $50 an hour, I wasn't about to blow my meager funds on idle con-
versation with a shrink. As it was, it had taken a carload of courage
for me just to make the appointment. All I needed from Dr. Brady
were some simple tips I could apply to my life immediately. Within
minutes a portly, bearded gentleman ushered me into his office and
motioned me to a leather seat that faced his high-backed swivel chair.
"Make yourself comfortable," he said. "What brings you in?"

I took a deep breath and then poured out the chronology of
events that led to our meeting. "Eighteen years ago I married a man
I adored," I said. "But from the start we were never close like a husband and wife should be. He's a very private person. I feel alone, and
so do our kids. We've had money problems from day one, and now
there's another woman and he wants to leave. What should I do?" I
caught my breath, sat back, and waited for the solution. I pulled out
a pen and small pad from my purse. I was certain his advice would
fit on a Post-it Note.

"How do you feel about this?" Dr. Brady asked.

I squirmed in my chair. "What do you mean?"

"I'm wondering what it feels like to be mistreated, to be in debt, to
watch your kids hurting, and to be shoved aside for another woman."

Gosh! Hearing a perfect stranger summarize my troubles in a

one-sentence list sent my mind reeling. "I don't know how I feel," I
said, surprised by his question. I had come in looking for an answer
not expecting to give one. "No one's ever asked me that before. I've
just tried to do what's right, but now I don't know what the right
thing is. That's why I'm here. I want you to tell me."

Dr. Brady pulled his chair forward. "I don't have the answer," he
said slowly, "but there is one. And you'll find it as we work together,
but it may take some time."

My pulse jumped and my palms moistened. *Time and money! I
should have known he's going to try to drag this out.* "I don't have time.
My husband is about to take off. He can't. He just can't!" I broke
down and sobbed. "I miss him, and the kids need their dad. How
can I make him stay?"

Dr. Brady was as calm as the sky after a rainstorm. "You may not
be able to," he said. Then he waited.

That was not what I wanted to hear.

He leaned over and looked me in the eyes. "But you can discover
what's right for you and for your children. Let's focus on that."

"Okay." My voice sounded weak to my ears. I didn't know where
else to turn, so I made another appointment and another and
another. As I continued my work with Dr. Brady, we got to the
point where he asked about my spiritual life and what I knew about
God. I didn't see what any of that had to do with my troubled marriage. In fact, I was annoyed by the question. From what I knew,
God was in heaven and I was on earth. And that was that.

Over time, Dr. Brady showed me that the hole in my soul had
been there long before I married my husband. In his wisdom, Dr.
Brady didn't try to persuade me to look into Judaism, his faith, or
to steer me to any other religious practice. He trusted that I would
find my own way.

I'd been raised in a legalistic home and church where rules
seemed more important than relationships. I was told what to do,
and I did it. Once again I expected that same formula to work. Find
out the rules for putting my marriage and family back together and
then follow them. That is, until I began to see that this situation
required more than a pat formula.

My husband already had one foot out the door and the other

close behind. My children were confused and frightened, and I was on the verge of a breakdown. I was sick to my stomach almost every day, could hardly sleep, and was overwhelmed with unmanageable debt. My husband had purchased a ranch for an investment and a small airplane without consulting me. I didn't have a job, nor was I in any condition to look for one. I felt trapped.

The harder I tried to appeal to my husband and calm my children's fears, the more apparent it was that I couldn't do this on my own power. I was in way over my head. I realized that discovering the truth about my own feelings was only the first step. And that would mean nothing unless I also discovered the truth about God—that he was the only one who had the answers I needed.

I stopped counseling after two years and took up a quest for God that led me to a variety of churches, seminars, recorded messages, and books. I prayed as well as I knew how and joined a Bible study. I remember being especially struck by the Gospel of John and its message that Jesus Christ was and is the Son of God.

Then one chilly Tuesday morning in December, the year after I ended my sessions with Dr. Brady, I came to the end of myself while returning from a walk on the beach. By then I had moved out of the family home and lived in an apartment. Nothing made sense anymore. I sat down right where I was and sobbed. "God, who are you? Where are you? Do you care anything about me? I've tried to find you. I want to know you."

Seconds passed. Then ever so gently a stream of familiar words from John's Gospel came to mind: "I am the way and the truth and the life. No one comes to the Father except through me" (14:6). I began shaking. I had read these words of Jesus Christ dozens of times. *Why do they sound so different now?* I wondered. Then I knew. I'd never let them in before. I'd never heard them in relation to *my* life. But that day I did. I jumped up and whirled around. "Jesus Christ is the way to God!" I shouted. And to think I almost missed him. No "higher power," no "life force," and no "spiritual guide" had ever offered me such assurance. Everything was new in that moment. I was no longer a victim of my husband's painful actions against me. Paul taught, "All have sinned and fall short of the glory of God" (Romans 3:23). Jesus became the sacrifice for my sin by his death on the cross. I could hardly take it in. And by his resurrection from the dead, I am assured of eternal life.

No wonder I hadn't fully received this gift before. I hadn't seen myself as a sinner because I was too preoccupied with the sins others had committed against me. But that day I knew I needed forgiveness as much as anyone. Christ didn't come for the righteous, but rather to give sinners an opportunity to repent and follow him (Matthew 9:13). I was a sinner, and I prayed that day for forgiveness as I put my faith and trust in Jesus Christ as my Lord and Savior. "Whoever hears my word and believes him who sent me has eternal life and will not be judged but has crossed over from death to life" (John 5:24). I began my new life that day.

Decades have passed since that Tuesday afternoon when I first walked into Dr. Brady's office. The answers I'd looked for then didn't come the way I'd hoped or expected, but they did come. My husband left and didn't come back. But Christ came in the nick of time, and he has never left my side!

Start by doing what's necessary; then do what's possible; and suddenly you are doing the impossible.

St. Francis of Assisi

Cousin Harry

Blessed is the one who trusts in the LORD,
whose confidence is in him.
JEREMIAH 17:7

Harry Flowers, my husband's colorful cousin, was famous for his corny humor, tall tales, and inspiring sermons. He was a church pastor before he retired in the 1980s. Years later, over breakfast at the Cracker Barrel Old Country Store and Restaurant in Paducah, Kentucky, Harry regaled family members with a story that at first sounded like another tall tale. After a few sentences, I was hooked on the story…as well as on the man himself.

"It was my habit," he began, "to sit in my favorite chair each morning and pray over my day." One Thursday, just after Harry said "Amen," the word "chicken" crossed his mind. "I wondered what that was about," he said, scratching the side of his head, "so I thought, 'All right. I'll order some fried chicken and see where this leads.'" He asked God for guidance. Without it he'd have a few cooked birds on his hands and a lot of explaining to do when he saw his wife, Anne, that evening.

He reached for the phone to call Redman's Barbecue and place his order, when suddenly he remembered Bill only barbecued chickens on Tuesdays. Harry called anyway, on the chance that the schedule might have changed. Bill answered the phone. When he heard Harry's request, he let out a soft laugh. "Good timing, friend. As a matter of fact, the chickens came in later than usual this week, so we cooked 'em today!"

"Hot dog!" Harry thought. He rubbed his hands together, smiled, and placed an order for 12 chickens. He had no good reason for ordering a dozen. It just seemed like the thing to do at the time. A little later, he jumped into his car and dashed off to Bill's. He plopped his money on the counter and called out his order. "I'm here to pick up the 12 chickens for Harry Flowers!"

As Bill boxed up his order, Harry turned to the Lord in prayer, wondering what God wanted him to do with all that chicken. After getting the order, Harry carried it to the car, got in, turned the engine over, and headed out. "I turned onto one street and then another within a two-mile radius of the restaurant. I stopped at whatever house I felt led to. I took a chance each time by walking up to the door and knocking. When someone answered, I handed over a chicken or two—depending on what seemed right. I also told the person that God loved him or her."

Harry was quick to acknowledge that he was as perplexed by the circumstance as anyone, but he'd never known the Lord to fail him, so he kept on going, following the nudges as he felt them.

He was surprised by the welcome he received at every home. He hadn't known any of the people before that morning, but not a one turned him away or looked at him as though he'd lost his mind. Every person Harry encountered was desperate in one way or another, and he or she was completely grateful when he handed over a plump chicken fresh from the barbecue spit. Some had been praying that very morning for an answer to their need, whether it was for food, money, or medicine.

"At the first house," said Harry, "a man and his wife were in their eighties. She had a heart condition so was unable to shop or cook, and he'd just come home from the hospital that very day." They received the barbecued chicken from Harry with tears in their eyes.

Next he met a woman whose husband had left her and their three children. She had no food or money. "I left her $20 and two chickens."

At the third house, he provided for a retired school principal, who had heart and eye problems, and his wife, who was suffering with the flu.

"The last family didn't have enough food either, but one of the adults admitted he'd been too proud to ask for help," said Harry.

"By the time I drove home, I was out of chickens even though I had planned to keep one for my wife and me. When I told Anne what happened, she just smiled. She knew a thing or two about the man she'd been married to for more than 40 years."

Harry opened the pantry, looked around, and then turned to Anne. He said with a chuckle, "Looks like tonight it's going to be Dinty Moore Stew and saltine crackers."

That was fine with Anne. That evening over their modest meal, the pair had tears in their eyes over how God used Harry that day to meet the needs of so many needy hearts.

❧

Perfection is not attainable, but if we chase
perfection we can catch excellence.

Vince Lombardi

You don't have to analyze the entire journey ahead. All you have to do is concentrate on the next step, then the next, and then the next. If you want a mountaintop experience, if you want to rise above your life's circumstances, God is probably not going to send you an elevator. He will simply walk with you, guiding you one step at a time.

Linda Evans Shepherd,
When You Don't Know What to Pray

The Freeway—His Way

*We know that in all things God works for the good of those who
love him, who have been called according to his purpose.*
ROMANS 8:28

"As I eased onto the freeway one balmy Sunday evening," said
Marilyn, "I breathed a sigh of relief. The traffic was flowing smoothly.
That meant I'd get to the evening service at church on time. Buying
gas and running a few errands had taken all my cash, but I didn't
worry. God always provided what I needed."

Marilyn turned the stereo to her favorite Christian music station and relaxed. There were no traffic jams. She might even get to
church early, allowing her time to maneuver her walker into the
sanctuary without having to deal with a crowd of people.

"I relished the thought of the service ahead," she said. "The prayer
time would be a great opportunity to praise God for all his care
and to ask for help with my finances. As an invalid on a limited
income, any additional expenses created a real challenge. In fact,
I needed money right then for another prescription. I wondered
where it would come from." Marilyn threw up a prayer. "You know
the answer, dear Lord, even if I don't. So I'll trust you to provide."

Just then the traffic slowed down. Marilyn saw red taillights on
cars in all four lanes on her side of the freeway. "Not a good sign!
Assuming there must be an accident ahead, I turned off the stereo and began praying for anyone who might have been involved.
Then I asked God to help me get to church on time." Soon after,

traffic came to a complete standstill. Marilyn glanced at her watch and realized it was just about time for the service to start. "I was going to miss the music and praise and worship time. I'd also miss meeting and greeting everyone around me. It didn't seem fair."

After a long wait, a highway patrolman directed Marilyn to turn her car onto the road's shoulder. A large truck had jackknifed and spilled bales of hay across the entire road. "By the time I reached the church building, and parked in my usual handicapped spot by the front door, I was already an hour late. The ushers quietly helped me find the only seat left where I could park my walker without someone tripping over it." Marilyn nodded to the young man beside her when she sat down, but since the sermon had begun she didn't introduce herself.

"At the end of the message I greeted my pew mate. He smiled in return and gestured to my walker. 'Do you need help, ma'am?' he asked. I replied, 'No, thank you, dear. My walker will get me down the aisle, and I'm parked right by the front door, so I'll do just fine.'"

The young man hesitated and then spoke up. "Umm, that's not what I mean. Do you need my help financially?"

Marilyn stared at this complete stranger in disbelief. "No, thank you," she replied firmly, eager now to get out of the pew as quickly as possible.

"Please don't be embarrassed," he said. "God has put this need on my heart, so I want to obey him and help you." He looked inside his wallet and then smiled wryly. "I don't seem to have much cash myself tonight. But if you have a bank account, I'd like to write you a check."

At that point Marilyn wasn't sure what to do. "Well, okay. Thank you." She did need money, and she had asked God for help.

"He pulled out his checkbook, wrote me a check, folded it, and placed it in my hand," said Marilyn. "He said, 'God bless you, dear,' then he slipped into the crowd. By then my curiosity was getting the best of me. I could hardly wait to walk outside and take a look at the amount."

Marilyn's car was one of the last remaining in the parking lot, and it was already dark. Her car ceiling light was broken. "How in the world can I look at the check?" she asked herself. "Fortunately,

I remembered my trusty flashlight in the glove compartment. I turned it on and held it over the check. I had expected an amount of $5, or $10, or maybe $20. Instead it was for $2000!"

"Oh, thank you, thank you, Jesus!" I shouted. The following day, Marilyn cashed the check, and it went through without a problem. "With careful budgeting and planning, it helped meet my needs for a long, long time," she said. "I was able to use part of it to make a thanks offering to God."

From the traffic jam on the freeway, to the overturned truck, and to her late arrival at church, it was clear to Marilyn that God had used all of these circumstances to have her arrive at just the right time so she would sit by the young man the Holy Spirit was going to use to provide for her needs. Truly, God's ways are higher than our ways.

Things turn out best for the people who make
the best out of the way things turn out.

Art Linkletter

More Than a Miracle

*The one who believes in me will live, even though they die;
and whoever lives by believing in me will never die.*
JOHN 11:25-26

Dorcas, a widow who lived in the coastal town of Joppa, an old city on the Mediterranean Sea about 30 miles northwest of Jerusalem, was known for her generous acts of charity. Everyone who knew this kind woman loved and esteemed her. One day she became ill. Most likely her friends and family did all they could to nurse her back to health. In ancient times there were no hospitals or medical clinics as we know them. Despite the care she received, Dorcas died. Those who attended her washed her body, as was the custom, and laid her out in the upper room of her house—a space set apart from the ground-floor public rooms and courtyard. For many people, the upper room was usually a place for quiet and prayer.

Friends and family members displayed their respect by grieving openly, which was part of the mourning ritual of that time and place. They cried and wailed, and some even tore parts of their woven garments to show their level of grief.

One person in the crowd gathered around the body had an idea. Hearing that the apostle Peter was in nearby Lydda, two men were dispatched to go to him. Ask if he'll come at once, they were told.

When the two men arrived, Peter responded right away. He set off on the 12-mile walk to Joppa. When he arrived, he was ushered into the room where Dorcas's body lay. Friends came forward to show him the garments Dorcas had made for the poor, and they likely talked about what a good life she'd lived and how she was always thinking of others before herself.

Peter was so moved by their sharing and expressions of deep grief over their loss that he wanted to do something to comfort them. He sent them outside the room so peace and quiet could be restored. Then he knelt and prayed, facing away from the body. Perhaps he wanted to focus his entire attention on God and the petition that was on his lips. Feeling the expectations of those waiting downstairs, he might have broken out in a sweat or felt the strong beat of his heart. He surely knew the Lord would answer his prayer, but maybe not in the way he hoped. So much depended on that moment.

Friends and family were probably bubbling with anticipation of what he might do, eager for a miracle yet unsure of the outcome. They'd already endured a long wait while the messengers went to get him and then while Peter walked the 12 miles to reach Joppa. Was it possible his arrival would be in vain? Would they be disappointed? Dorcas's body was already cold and would soon start to decay.

After praying, Peter turned toward Dorcas's body. Calling the woman by her Jewish name, Tabitha, he drew on the same divine power Jesus had, commanding her to come back to life. "Tabitha, get up." And Tabitha opened her eyes, looked at Peter, and sat up. He reached out his hand and raised her to a standing position. What gratitude he must have felt that God had answered him with awesome power. Then he called for Tabitha's friends so they could see what had happened. Not only had the woman they loved been restored to life, but she was restored to their community as well.

The Christians of his time were inspired and encouraged by the event. The young church expanded and grew because of this miracle. As for Peter, he was transformed in that moment too. Up to that point he saw his mission as bringing the gospel of Jesus Christ to the Jewish people. But on this day he experienced a new dimension for his life and for human history. In a dream that followed shortly after that experience, he realized he was to also reach out to Gentiles for Christ.

⁓

Thank God for little miracles, right?
Michael Bergin

Green Shoes

The LORD is good and his love endures forever;
his faithfulness continues through all generations.
PSALM 100:5

"We haff no money for food! Ve must pray!" Pastor René recounts vividly these words his mother spoke with her thick, Swiss-German accent when things were desperate for her and her two children after her husband died. "I remember holding hands in our kitchen, a little circle of three," said René. "We asked God, quite literally, for our daily bread." The small family lived under the poverty line for eight years. "But God always provided," he added, and often in the nick of time. "Although not always in the way I would have preferred," he admitted.

For example, in one prayer they asked specifically for milk. The very next morning they found a box of powdered milk on their doorstep. René said he couldn't stand powdered milk, but it provided what they needed. "To this day I have no idea how it got there or who donated it," he said.

On another occasion the family prayed for shoes for René— and on the following day shoes just his size were left in a bag on the porch. René laughed as he related the story. "They were the ugliest, puke-green shoes I'd ever seen in my life." He told his mother vehemently there was no way he'd wear them to school. She replied in no uncertain terms, "You vill wear zem!" And so he did. To René's surprise, the kids thought they were cool! "That sure felt good."

These and many other last-minute answers to prayer made a deep impression on young René. In fact, they affected him to such an extent that as an adult he feels passionate about feeding the hungry, particularly those who lack even the basics, such as milk and bread.

One day while preparing to speak at a funeral for a man who was about the same age as René's father when he died, René turned to his mother for wisdom. He wanted to pass on to the widow and mother of two young children a message that would encourage and comfort them in their grief. Who better to advise him than his mother who clearly understood what the family was going through?

She paused for a moment and then said four little-but-powerful words: "The Lord will provide." She had seen evidence of his provision again and again in her life as a single mother.

René and his mom enjoyed recalling more of the ways God had literally put food on their table and shoes on their feet in the nick of time.

The richness of the human experience would lose something of rewarding joy if there were no limitations to overcome.

Helen Keller

Walkin' in the Rain

[The LORD] gives strength to the weary
and increases the power of the weak.
ISAIAH 40:29

"It's now or never," I muttered as I gazed at the highest point of Mount Whitney I could see from where I stood. At 14,497 feet, Whitney is the tallest mountain in the Continental United States. The following day I was going to hike to the top with three women friends, each named Betty. At age 57, I knew this was my last chance. I couldn't imagine waiting another year.

We had just come off a weeklong trek and campout at 10,000 feet, so we were acclimated to high elevation and had built up our stamina. The night before, we booked a room at the Dow Villa Hotel in Lone Pine, California, a small town at the foot of the mountain and the site of many western movies from the thirties and forties.

After a meal of pizza and salad at a local café, we returned to our room to load our backpacks with the essentials for our journey. Just before collapsing on our cots, we did a final inspection, each one holding up the item and calling out "check."

- Food and small cookstove
- Spare clothes
- Sun hat, sunglasses, and sunscreen
- Tent, poles, camp mattress, and sleeping bag

- Hiking sticks
- Raingear and gloves

Three "checks" echoed across the room…but there were four of us.

Betty S. remained silent as she rummaged through her pack while we waited. Then, with a sigh of relief, she held up one leg of her waterproof pants. "Check!" she said. "All here."

I slipped in and out of sleep all night, fear and excitement tumbling through my stomach. The next morning we arose early, showered (the last time for the next three days), ate a quick breakfast, grabbed our gear, and set out on this trip we had organized over a year ago. We hadn't planned for snow, though we had plenty of clothing just in case.

As we looked at the slope above us and just below the summit, there it was. Snow packed so thick and so hard that it wiped out any signs of the 92-step switchback trail. We had to plunge our poles and booted feet into the deep drifts, one agonizing step at a time until we reached the ridge below the peak.

Two hours later we hit the narrow trail to the summit and paused to take deep breaths. We were hungry and exhausted but also exhilarated. I spotted the small stone hut at the top, a welcome sight! We trekked up to the enclosure and posed in front of it for a photo with a banner we'd prepared ahead of time. "Karen and the three Bettys made it to the top of Mount Whitney!"

After a rest and some food, we started down, eager to reach our campground for the night. We would complete the trip to the bottom the following day. The descent was treacherous as we placed one foot in front of the other on the narrow trail between two steep slopes that would have sent us to our deaths if we missed our footing. Not a word was exchanged as we concentrated. I prayed—and hoped the others were doing the same. Then, without warning, a fierce rainstorm swept in. It was so strong and mighty that we were forced to stop on the muddy trail and don our raingear. Within minutes three of us were bundled up, hoods in place, and waterproof gloves covering our woolen mittens.

Betty S. screeched! "Where's my jacket?" She ransacked her pack but it was nowhere to be found. She'd brought the pants but failed to make sure the jacket was there too. None of us had a spare to loan her.

Shivering, she hurried ahead, the wind beating her face and neck as the rain soaked her fleece jacket. Up ahead, as if dropped from heaven, we spotted something shiny and yellow at the side of the trail. Upon closer inspection, it was a perfectly good yellow rain slicker, the kind kids wear to school and construction workers don during rain. I snatched it up and held it out to Betty.

She shook it out, slipped it on, and pulled the hood over her hat. We laughed and cried. A miracle! God had answered my prayer for protection and care as we walked down the trail. I never expected such a desperately needed item to appear in such an out-of-the-way place. But we can't put anything over on God. When he says he'll provide, he keeps his word in the nick of time.

Take the first step in faith. You don't have to see
the whole staircase, just take the first step.
Martin Luther King, Jr.

Christmas Coal

Have mercy on me, Lord.
PSALM 41:4

On Christmas morning, 1912, in Paducah, Kentucky, 14-year-old Charlie Flowers and his three brothers and two sisters huddled in their beds, fully dressed, trying to keep warm as the wind howled outside their small-frame house. It was a desperate time for the family. Earlier that year, the children's father had died, and their mother had not yet found work. The coal had run out, and they had very little money. Gifts were out of the question. A local merchant had given them a scrawny tree the night before. "Can't sell this one," the man said with a nod before handing it over to the eager children. The children had decorated it with scraps of colored paper.

To pass the time, the siblings joked and shouted stories from their bedrooms across the hallway from one another. Then suddenly a racket from the alley at the rear of the house broke into their games.

"Charlie!" his mother called. "Will you see what's going on out there?"

Charlie pulled on his shoes, grabbed a thick overcoat from a hook by the door, and ran out back. There stood a man in a wagon bent over a load of coal, shoveling it into the shed as fast as he could.

"Hey, mister, we didn't order any coal," Charlie shouted. "You're delivering it to the wrong house."

"Your name's Flowers, isn't it?" the man asked, still shoveling.

Charlie nodded.

"Well, there's no mistake. I've been asked to deliver this to your family on Christmas morning." He looked the awestruck boy squarely in the eyes. "And I'm under strict orders not to tell who sent it," he added.

Charlie ran into the house, his coattail flapping in the cold, morning wind. He could hardly wait to tell his mother, brothers, and sisters. God had answered their prayers for help. He'd provided—just as he had on that first Christmas morning so long ago when he sent his only son to a needy world. They would now have a cozy fire to enjoy! And Mother could make tea and toast. They would celebrate Christmas after all.

Charlie Flowers died in 1994 at age 96. Right up to the last year of his life, not a Christmas went by that he didn't tell the story of that sub-zero Christmas morning in his boyhood when two men gave his family an unforgettable and much-needed gift. It wasn't the coal that was remembered or cherished, Charlie often said, as welcome as it was. Rather, it's what the two men brought to the desperate family. One blessing was from the one who had a gift for recognizing the great need and then took the time to do something about it. And the other was for the man willing to give up part of his Christmas morning to deliver it.

That gift of coal so long ago continues to warm the Flowers family reunions as it's passed on from one generation to another. Charlie's son, my husband Charles, shares about these two strangers each Christmas and whispers "thanks" to God for answering his family's prayer in the nick of time.

Gratitude is the rosemary of the heart.
Minna Antrim

Unceasing Prayer

You will pray to him, and he will hear you,
and you will fulfill your vows.
JOB 22:27

In ancient Israel, people believed that a large family was a sign of God's blessing. Hannah longed to be a mother, and she often wondered why she couldn't conceive while her husband's other wife seemed to bear children easily.

The second wife also enjoyed taunting Hannah over her barrenness until she wept and could hardly eat. Years went by, and the provocation continued. Hannah grew weary, but she *never* gave up praying for a child. She was focused and diligent, believing with her whole heart that God would honor her request. If he blessed her with a son, she promised to give the boy back to him through service in the temple.

One day while praying at the house of the Lord in Shiloh, Hannah was so intent that her lips mouthed her words to God. Eli the priest accused her of drinking too much. Hannah told him she was not drunk. Instead, she was pouring out her soul to the Lord.

Eli was touched by her words and obvious pain. "Go in peace," he responded, "and may the God of Israel grant you what you have asked of him" (1 Samuel 1:17).

That night after Hannah and her husband, Elkanah, returned to their home in Ramah, they slept together. Would this be the night? Would God answer her unceasing prayer? She wanted to

please Elkanah and her extended family with news that sh
pregnant. She also might have been thinking of the promise s.
made to God if he blessed her with a son. To Hannah's delig.
God answered her faithful prayers. She became pregnant and, nine
months later, gave birth to a son she named Samuel "because I asked
the LORD for him."

Even though God had been silent regarding Hannah's request for
many years, she never stopped praying. And just as she vowed, she
handed her young son over to Eli to be trained as a priest. "Pardon
me, my lord," she said to Eli at the temple. "As surely as you live, I
am the woman who stood here beside you praying to the LORD. I
prayed for this child, and the LORD has granted me what I asked of
him. So now I give him to the LORD. For his whole life he will be
given over to the LORD."

The conception of Samuel was not a day or year too early or too
late. God had chosen Samuel before the beginning of time to play
an important role as an adult in uniting the tribes of Israel against
the growing threat of the Philistines, to anoint Saul as king of Israel,
and, later in Bethlehem, to anoint David as Saul's successor.

God blessed Hannah for honoring her pledge. She bore three
more sons and two daughters!

Pray, and let God worry.
Martin Luther

We have heard it before, but we need to hear it very definitely—the condition of God's blessing is absolute surrender of all into His hands. Praise God! If our hearts are willing for that, there is no end to what God will do for us, and to the blessing God will bestow...Have you never yet learned the lesson that the Holy Ghost works with mighty power, while on the human side everything appears feeble?

Andrew Murray,
Absolute Surrender

Death's Door

Though outwardly we are wasting away,
yet inwardly we are being renewed day by day.
2 Corinthians 4:16

"Mom, I feel like I'm dying."

Sandra heard these chilling words from her daughter Dawn, who was 27 and expecting her second child. "Please pray for me. When I stand up, everything turns black. My heart is racing even while sitting down." Her daughter's plea drove Sandra to her knees. While at work, teaching first grade at a school in San Diego, California, when the kids were busy with projects she'd move to the back of the room and quietly pray with Dawn whenever she called.

Within weeks Dawn's condition grew worse. She couldn't lift her head or arms and was unable to walk. Her husband had to carry her up and down three flights of stairs to take her to and from medical appointments. But the examinations revealed nothing. Doctors couldn't find anything wrong with her. One even suggested she see a psychiatrist.

"I pleaded with Dawn to go to The Center for Advanced Medicine, where she could meet with medical doctors, chemists, and naturopaths," Sandra shared. Finally Dawn agreed. After a series of extensive tests, she was diagnosed with toxic metal poisoning and fungus. They also found that her system lacked some good bacteria common to humans.

Dawn gained very little weight during her pregnancy because

.er body couldn't absorb nutrients. She complained to her mother about being hungry and thirsty no matter what she ate or drank. Sandra prayed with her daughter daily, sometimes several times a day, and Dawn began a course of treatment to combat the symptoms.

"I read Psalm 91 and Ephesians 6:10-18, morning, noon, and night," Sandra confessed. "I looked for healing Scriptures and inserted Dawn's name in each one. I also prayed with my 85-year-old prayer partner throughout the entire pregnancy. I anointed my daughter's head with oil and praised God for the answer I knew would come—a healthy mom and a healthy baby."

Intercessors from all around the country prayed with and for Dawn for months. "We all stood on the promises of God, believing that if we had even the faith of a mustard seed we could move this mountain of fear and worry and illness."

A month or so before Dawn's baby was due, Sandra felt certain of the Lord's assurance that Dawn would have the strength to deliver a healthy baby despite the obstetrician's prediction that if she wasn't strong enough he'd have to vacuum the baby out. "Such a statement terrified us!" said Sandra. "But God answered our prayers in the nick of time. Even though my daughter was still in a weakened state, God gave her the stamina she needed to deliver Daniel Isaiah (10 pounds, 9 ounces) without intervention." Her labor lasted just two and a half hours.

"Without a doubt, this event was a miracle that could only come from God!" Sandra exclaimed. "And we give him all the glory!" Sandra took away from this experience a valuable lesson. "Our words can activate fear, doubt, and worry or they can ignite our faith. I learned to stand on God's healing promises and to speak words of life even when the condition seemed impossible."

God taught Sandra to speak to the mountain instead of to the condition. She held on firmly to the Lord and listened intently for his wisdom, guidance, and words of encouragement. "By the time Dawn delivered her baby," said Sandra, "God had done a very powerful work in our family. And he continued to do so as Dawn grew stronger over the following year of treatment when she was restored to complete health.

"I can't begin to tell you how listening to the dramatized version of the Bible on CD by Alexander Scourby made the Word of God come alive for me. My faith runs deeper now, and when the treacherous waters come, I am far more stable than ever before. I turned to Christ from Judaism when I was 28 years old. Today, at age 62, I really understand how God shapes our lives when we love him, lean on him, read his Word, and bend our will to his."

The greatest inspiration is often born of desperation.
Comer Cotrell

Persistence

*Consider it pure joy, my brothers and sisters, whenever you
face trials of many kinds, because you know that
the testing of your faith produces perseverance.*
JAMES 1:2-3

Ginger and her husband were living in Southern California when their first child was born. "Until that moment, I had planned to go right back to my well-paid, full-time job," said Ginger. "But when the time came, I suddenly realized I didn't want to leave my daughter with strangers. On the other hand, to give up my job would mean we'd have to live on half our previous income. I didn't know how we could, but I felt God wanted us to make that sacrifice." With trepidation, Ginger and Jim prayed for reassurance that the Lord would help them make it work.

Ginger's parents were thrilled about the arrival of their first grandchild. They lived in Northern California at the time and wanted the young family to move closer to them. The grandparents had purchased 30 acres of land and started a plant nursery out in the country.

When the couple learned their daughter wanted to stay home with the baby, they invited her and Jim to move north and settle on their land in a mobile home. "My dad helped Jim contact local companies for a job. Nothing turned up for nine months. We managed on the extra income from several small part-time jobs I picked

124

up," said Ginger. "Then one day Jim received an offer from a company located near my parents' property. We considered that God's confirmation. We moved in the spring of 1989 and started a brand-new chapter in our lives."

Jim and Ginger had grown up in suburbia, so country living was a new experience—and not always hunky-dory, as Ginger put it. "Soon after we arrived, a neighboring farmer came around a blind corner in his pickup on the narrow, winding dirt road between our properties. He ran head-on into our two-year-old car."

The police refused to investigate or report the collision since it occurred on private property. The insurance representatives considered it a case of Jim's word against the word of the other driver, so the couple had to pay the deductible to get the car repaired. At least it hadn't been totaled.

"A few months later, the Loma Prieta earthquake struck our county and caused enormous emotional trauma as well as physical damage," Ginger shared. "My dad's water tank broke, and we all had to work hard in unseasonable heat to save the nursery business. The upside is that this experience helped bond us to my parents."

The following winter was so cold the couple turned on the heat every day to keep the house warm for their little daughter, who was now crawling. "In February, when the propane tank had to be refilled, we were shocked by the astronomical bill. Money was very tight," Ginger shared. "And we didn't have nearly enough saved up to pay it." There was nothing they could do except pray. "I simply told God that my parents had already done so much to help us move in, and they had big expenses of their own after the earthquake so I didn't want to ask them for a loan." She leaned on the Lord for an answer and solution.

Ginger felt bad that they were unprepared for what should have been an expected household expense. "I had only begun to live for Christ three years before," she said, "so I was still immature in my faith. This was one of the first big financial tests we had gone through since I gave up my job to stay home with the baby. The bill was due in two weeks, and I worried and stressed constantly. With fear and anger I questioned God. 'Why did you let this happen? What are we supposed to do now?'

Days later, just before the payment was due, a check arrived in the mail from the auto insurance company. According to the letter that accompanied the money, the other driver's insurance company had agreed to pay for the damage caused by the collision. That meant Jim and Ginger were entitled to a refund of part of their deductible.

Ginger reflected on this season in their lives. "I learned that God has good reasons for allowing difficulties, such as the accident expense, and sometimes even shows how that challenge will turn out for my best." She realized that if she and Jim hadn't paid that deductible eight months before, they probably wouldn't have had that amount saved for the propane bill. "God is faithful to provide what we need, and my worrying doesn't help. I need to wait patiently for his answer, and then I need to encourage others by sharing how he provided."

Since that experience, Jim and Ginger have endured many other financial tests, including three job layoffs. "We always saw God come through, often in the nick of time," shared Ginger. "I trust him more and more each year."

Adopt the pace of nature: her secret is patience.

Ralph Waldo Emerson

Learning Curve

*The LORD your God will bless you
in the land he is giving you.*
DEUTERONOMY 28:8

"In 2010, while trying to sell our condo, my wife and I found a great deal on a new house that met every want and need we'd put before God," Simon Presland shared. "After praying, Trish and I felt we couldn't pass it up, so we made an offer that was accepted within two weeks." The couple was ecstatic and incredibly grateful to God. Escrow would close in six weeks. In the meantime, they'd have to carry two mortgages until their condo sold.

"Four offers on the place fell through, some all cash, over the next several months due to one mishap and another. When we were in the last week of our three-month window for being able to manage two house payments, a woman in an adjacent condo approached us about renting ours. She had been living with her boyfriend, but they were now splitting up."

Simon and Trish had openly shared their faith with the couple and helped them at times with chores around the house. They even dog sat for them when they were away. "We felt this opportunity to rent our condo was God's way of giving us extra time to sell it," said Simon, "so we said yes."

However, the woman couldn't afford to pay the equivalent of the couple's mortgage, so Simon and Trish made up the difference out of their own pockets. This presented a new challenge. "During this period, we went through every emotion possible," Simon shared. "Anxiety over keeping the condo clean and ready for viewing, worries over having sufficient finances to carry both loans, concern that either home might need a major repair, fear that we might have jumped ahead of God, euphoria when we received an offer on the condo, and heartache each time a sale fell through. Yes, we were grateful at first, but after a few weeks we became a bit discouraged. The way things were going didn't seem fair." Then they decided to put a stop to that mind-set. They chose to pray particular verses of Scripture throughout the week for God's will to be done. "We didn't know if we were to take action or stay put, and we certainly didn't want to pay two mortgages. As we continued to pray 'thy will be done' throughout the house-hunting and condo-selling process, we were amazed at how God's will unfolded as we shared our faith with our neighbor and with our real estate agent."

Within weeks the neighbor started attending church. One day she gave her life to Christ! "Two weeks after that, a buyer came along, offered to pay us cash for our condo as an investment, and said our neighbor could continue renting as long as she wanted to."

Simon said this experience showed them without a doubt that God really does honor faith. "We also learned that his will can include answering prayer in a way that is far better than what we ask or imagine, just like it says in Ephesians 3:19-21." They saw for themselves that no one can customize prayers to bring about a certain result. "God can take you on a roller coaster ride," said Simon, "but he'll get you to where he wants you to go as long as you're open and willing to accept his answer—which often comes in the nick of time, just as it did for us."

Simon said that today he doesn't stress over material things nearly as much as he once did. "I now have confidence in God's ability to answer prayer. I also see him as my father, a role I never understood until now. I have an underlying sense of peace that permeates my day-to-day life. I am fully convinced that God can do for others what he has done for Trish and me. When conflicts arise, I see them as part of his will and my learning curve instead of getting defensive and ending up in an argument. I am now growing through them instead of getting caught in them."

What you get by achieving your goals is not as important as what you become by achieving your goals.

Henry David Thoreau

Kindness Rewarded

The LORD is with me; he is my helper.
PSALM 118:7

A terrible famine overcame the town of Bethlehem during the period from 1250 to 1050 BC. People were desperate for food. A man named Elimelek, his wife, Naomi, and their sons, Mahlon and Kilion, moved away as quickly as they could and settled in the neighboring country of Moab.

According to what is written about them in the Bible's Old Testament, Elimelek died and the sons wedded two Moabite women. Mahlon married Ruth, and Kilion took Orpah for his wife. Tragedy struck again when these two men died. At that point, Elimelek's widow, Naomi, decided to return to her home in Bethlehem. Apparently she didn't want to stay in a foreign land without her husband and sons. She released her daughters-in-law from their familial obligations, advising them to go back to their own mothers and find new husbands. Reluctantly, Orpah left.

Ruth, however, replied with confidence, "Don't urge me to leave you or to turn back from you. Where you go I will go, and where you stay I will stay. Your people will be my people and your God my God. Where you die I will die, and there I will be buried. May the LORD deal with me, be it ever so severely, if even death separates you and me" (Ruth 1:16-17).

Naomi must have been startled by such a response, but I imagine it pleased her to hear she would have a lifetime companion. The two women arrived in Bethlehem after the famine had ended and about the time of the barley harvest. To support her mother-in-law and herself, Ruth went to the fields to collect the grain left in the fields after harvesting, a process called "gleaning."

A man named Boaz, a close relative of Naomi's husband's family and the owner of the land where Ruth was gleaning, saw Ruth picking up barley. He was kind to her, especially after learning of her loyalty to Naomi. With his permission, Ruth continued to glean from Boaz's fields for the remainder of the harvest.

Boaz, by his relationship to Elimelek, was in line to be obliged by Jewish (Levirate) law to marry Mahlon's widow, Ruth, to carry on the deceased man's family line. To make this happen quickly, Naomi sent Ruth to the threshing floor one night, telling her to "uncover the feet" of Boaz and lay down by them while he slept. Ruth obeyed. When Boaz awakened and asked, "Who are you?" it was probably dark. He must have wondered who would come to him in the middle of the night! Ruth identified herself, and asked Boaz to spread the corner of his garment over her because he was the guardian-redeemer of Elimelek's family. Spreading a cloak was a woman's way of asking for marriage back then. Boaz replied that he'd be willing to redeem Ruth by marriage, but there was one complication. Another male relative held the first right of redemption. Boaz said he would look into the situation.

The next morning, Boaz discussed the issue with the other relative in front of the town elders. The man was unwilling to jeopardize the inheritance of his estate by marrying Ruth, so he waived his right of redemption, which opened the way for Boaz to marry Ruth.

> (Now in earlier times in Israel, for the redemption and transfer of property to become final, one party took off his sandal and gave it to the other. This was the method of legalizing transactions in Israel.) So the guardian-redeemer said to Boaz, "Buy it yourself." And he removed his sandal. Then Boaz announced to the elders and all the people, "Today you are witnesses that I have bought from Naomi all

the property of Elimelek, Kilion and Mahlon. I have also acquired Ruth the Moabite, Mahlon's widow, as my wife, in order to maintain the name of the dead with his property, so that his name will not disappear from among his family or from his hometown. Today you are witnesses!" (Ruth 4:7-10).

Boaz and Ruth were married and had a son named Obed, who later became the grandfather of David, who became king of Israel.

Ruth played a vital role in the restoration of her mother-in-law Naomi. It doesn't say that Naomi prayed for Ruth to remain with her. In fact, she told Ruth to return to her own mother. But when Ruth refused to leave her, Naomi probably acknowledged her longing for companionship after the death of her husband. Perhaps she even prayed for it without anyone knowing except God.

Imagine how fearful and vulnerable she must have felt after losing her spouse and two sons and then facing the possibility of her daughters-in-law leaving as well. She may have been wary of asking Ruth and Orpah to stay with her because they were still young and could rebuild their lives with new husbands in their own country. She knew money would be tight, and how would all three of them live? Naomi, in her old age, also didn't want to be a burden to Ruth.

But God knew Naomi's heart, and he provided. He also looked out for Ruth, who must have been devastated by the loss of her husband and father-in-law. Two widows making their way in the world would have been very challenging, especially in that era. Ruth did what she felt was God's will. The Bible doesn't say she prayed, but I can picture her doing so. How else would she know the importance of staying with her mother-in-law? She does say Naomi's God will be her God. And Naomi's God was the one true God, the God of Abraham! Ruth did what she thought was right, and God took care of the rest.

Deliberately seek opportunities for kindness, sympathy, and patience.
Evelyn Underhill

Speaking Up

The LORD longs to be gracious to you;
therefore he will rise up to show you compassion.
ISAIAH 30:18

Lynn zipped into the far left lane of the freeway. She glanced at the clock on the dashboard and breathed a sigh of relief. She had an hour to make it to her destination—a Mothers of Preschoolers meeting (MOPS) at a church in a town about 40 miles north of where she lived. She turned on the car radio and selected her favorite classical music station. Just then the car in front of her flashed red lights. Lynn slammed on the brakes. *What happened?* she wondered. Traffic had been moving at a comfortable pace until then. She looked at her side mirror to see if she could move off the freeway and saw nothing but a long ribbon of red lights. "Oh great! Now I'll be late. How do I get out of this one?" she shrieked as she smacked her fist on the steering wheel. There was no way to move with cars stopped in all four lanes.

The speaker the meeting planner had booked initially had cancelled the day before due to breaking her leg. Lynn had agreed to replace her, and she was eager to speak to the group of young moms about how to maintain a joyful attitude even when things get tough. She took out her cell phone and called the woman in charge. "It looks like I'm going to be late—maybe as much as an hour, from what I can see by traffic on the freeway." She didn't like the sour tone in her voice, but at this point she couldn't help it.

The meeting planner was as gracious and cheerful as anyone could have wanted. She said she'd switch around the agenda, and Lynn could speak after the morning brunch and craft activity.

"Shame swept over me," said Lynn. "I was the one who was supposed to bring a message of hope and joy to the women, and I was anything but hopeful or joyful in that moment." She turned to God, asking him to keep her focused on him instead of the circumstances. There was nothing she could do about the traffic but wait it out. Inch by inch the cars began moving until her car reached the scene that had held up the flow. On the side of the road was a vehicle mangled from front to back, emergency vehicles, police, firefighters, and paramedics gathered around it.

"Once we passed, the traffic picked up again," Lynn said. "I was back on my way, but I was a different person than before. I couldn't help but think about the victims of that crash. Were they alive or dead? I might have been one of them had I reached that point before they did." Lynn continued her drive, praying for those involved in the wreck, for the women she was going to speak to, and for herself to arrive safely and in good spirits. She pulled into the church parking lot only 30 minutes late. When she walked into the meeting room, the moms were sitting at tables finishing their crafts and bubbling with conversation.

The meeting planner greeted Lynn with a warm hug and welcome. She introduced her to the group. Lynn opened her talk by sharing the experience she'd just had on the freeway—admitting her own self-centered thoughts before she realized the truth. "And here I was, on my way to encourage you to remain hopeful and joyful in *all* circumstances." She laughed. "I was hardly a model of what I had to say." Then she transitioned into her presentation, thanking God for being in control even if she didn't realize it until the nick of time.

You're just a prayer away from a change of heart.
Henry Brandt

Cancer Challenged

*My help comes from the LORD,
the Maker of heaven and earth.*
PSALM 121:2

In December of 2010, while undressing in the bathroom, Anita was startled to see a strange shape on the surface of her right breast. It was dark black in color but small in size, so she didn't give it further consideration. She got ready for bed and went back to studying for her German test. "I had to pass in order to get a student card that was required to obtain a residence permit in Germany," she said. "It was my last chance, so I was consumed with stressful thoughts about succeeding."

Four months later, after having passed the exam, the spot on her breast changed to an open wound, and it had grown. The pain increased to such a degree that she could sleep only two or three hours a night. She made an appointment to see a physician at a special hospital for women in the German city where she lived. "After the doctor saw the symptoms and took X-rays, he said, 'This could be breast cancer.' That scared me."

Anita endured several medical examinations before the physicians arrived at the correct diagnosis. "One week later, I returned to the hospital to hear the result. 'You have a malignant breast tumor,' he said, 'and it should be removed as soon as possible.'"

With God's help and good medical insurance, all the financial costs would be taken care of. Anita relied on the prayers of her family in Indonesia as she waited for the scheduled surgery two weeks later. "We asked God to strengthen my faith, for wisdom for all the doctors and nurses, and for peace that his will would be done."

Then the unexpected occurred. Three days before Anita's surgery, the doctor performed another medical test and decided to postpone the procedure, saying it was high risk and that it would be better to do six months of chemotherapy first. Anita's primary doctor then consulted with another physician. He expressed a different opinion, stating Anita could have her surgery the following Monday as originally planned.

Later the two physicians told Anita they would meet with the hospital's chief of staff before making a final decision. "When I heard all this," said Anita, "I could only surrender to God. I begged him to declare his will to the doctors." When more doubts arose, Anita prayed through them, and her family did the same. At times she was scared, but then she remembered that "with God there is no problem too big for him to handle. Whatever the state of my breast, I knew he would help me through it his way."

While waiting for the medical decision, Anita was tense with anxiety, remaining close to God in prayer. The doctors returned to her room and told her the chief of staff offered to do the surgery himself. "But you must wait one week, as he is now on vacation," said one of the doctors. Anita was also relieved to hear the man was highly skilled and experienced. She knew then God had answered her prayer by giving her the most qualified physician in the hospital.

"I am a humble foreign student in Germany," she said. "I could not have demanded that I have the best doctor. Only Jesus could do that for me—and he did." Once Anita knew that God's hand was in the decision to operate and he had selected the surgeon, she relaxed, believing the Lord would take care of all the other details and the procedure would be successful.

During that week, she and her family prayed together by phone, asking God for favor for everyone involved and trusting him to bring about the perfect outcome. On the day of surgery, "God lifted my fear of anesthesia," said Anita. "His peace allowed me to relax. During the journey from my room to the surgical suite, I was free of worry."

Three days later the surgeon visited Anita to share the results. "He was pleased with the outcome but admitted, 'While operating I had some difficulty, but we got past it.' When I heard that, my heart was filled with gratitude. What had been a challenge for the doctor was easy for Jesus Christ, who guided his hands."

Today Anita is more confident that God will never leave her because he loves her. "His time and his ways are always the best. I am not a strong person. Although at age 41 I am no longer a child, I have learned to live like a child in my relationship with God. He is the giver of life. Without him I can't do anything. My life depends solely on God's mercy, and as a result I am now calmer and more peaceful than ever, even as I go through a series of chemotherapy treatments. God took care of everything in the nick of time."

Life is 10% of what happens to me and 90% of how I react to it.
John Maxwell

Sometimes Luther had the temerity to undertake also the greater encounter with God himself. "I dispute much with God with great impatience," said he, "and I hold him to his promises." The Canaanite woman was a source of unending wonder and comfort to Luther because she had the audacity to argue with Christ. When she asked him to come and cure her daughter, he answered that he was not sent but to the lost sheep of the house of Israel, and that it was not meet to take the children's bread and give it to the dogs. She did not dispute his judgment. She agreed that she was a dog. She asked no more than that which befits a dog, to lick up the crumbs, which fall from the children's table. She took Christ at his own words. He then treated her not as a dog but as a child of Israel.

Roland H. Bainton,
Here I Stand: A Life of Martin Luther

Blooming Where Planted

In their hearts humans plan their course,
but the LORD establishes their steps.
PROVERBS 16:9

Unhappy in her teaching position at a college campus, Beth Young sought a position at a similar institution nearby. She received an offer for the following year. "I accepted it and then began filling out the paperwork to resign from my home campus. Something wasn't right though. I felt uneasy about the change, but for various reasons I judged it to be the will of God—a value that has been precious to me since I was a child."

Even so, Beth spent hours crying, praying internally and passionately, and laboring over her decision. She asked God for clarity and the courage to do the right thing no matter how she felt. "Time passed and the uncertainty continued," Beth said. "I longed for a definitive answer, and I could only trust my desire to do the will of God. Not knowing what else to do, I relied on the hope that direction would come, trusting my motivation and God's presence in partnership. I did not ask my community of friends and church to pray for and with me then, but I would do that today."

Beth's situation hit a crisis point when her three-year-old daughter asked, "Are you going to cry again today, Mommy?"

"I was shaken into the realization that I had lost my peace of mind and heart for weeks and my tears showed it. I panicked." Beth phoned her husband, Dan, for advice yet again. They had talked

over the situation many times. He admitted he didn't know what
more to say. "I want what's best for you," he said. He acknowledged
that only she knew what that was. He agreed to be flexible and
accepting either way.

"I called one more person—a teaching colleague," Beth said. "It's
my habit to consult with a lot of people when I'm trying to discern
important choices. This man had left our campus for another, and
he now judged it to be a mistake on his part. He advised me to listen to my anxiety and to withdraw from the new post if I regretted my acceptance. 'That could well be the most difficult phone call
you'll ever make,' he warned, 'but that's no reason not to make it.'"

That reflection rang true in Beth's heart. "I made that call, with-
drew from the new post, and tore up my resignation paperwork the
very day it was due! Fortunately, my secretary had purposely waited
to submit it at the last minute, hoping I wouldn't really leave. God
(and my secretary!) saved me in the nick of time."

Beth made a new decision—to bloom where she'd been planted.
"I also pledged to be open to change at a later time," she added.
"Within a few months, I was promoted at my home institution and
given new leadership in my department. I worked as the chairper-
son for more than two decades."

Beth did indeed bloom where she was planted!

"God speaks to me through my tears and anxiety, and through
the questions, advice, and hopes of other people," said Beth. "I
learned through this experience to listen well to my emotions and
to other people rather than only to what *I think* is God's will. We
see darkly, as Paul wrote in his letter to the Corinthians, and we
learn slowly."

Today, Beth is more willing to trust God's timing. "If I feel pres-
sured to make a decision, I tend to put it on hold, waiting for clarity and courage until the appropriate answer emerges. Then I feel
'right with God.'"

The harder the conflict, the more glorious the triumph.
Thomas Paine

Man of Faith

Faith is confidence in what we hope for
and assurance about what we do not see.
HEBREWS 11:1

During 1162 BC, the people of Israel began worshipping the storm god Baal with apparently little thought to how God would view it. So God left them to suffer the consequences of their sin.

At that time, the Midianites, who lived near the desert on the east side of Israel, came against the Jewish tribes in the middle of the country. The tribes of Ephraim and part of Manasseh on the western side of Jordan were hit the hardest. For seven years persecution swept across the land at harvest time, the invaders carrying away all the grain crops until the Israelites and their herds were without even a scrap of food.

In addition, the Midianites brought their flocks of sheep and camels to Israel and allowed them to eat all the grass in the fields. This drove the residents out of their villages and farms, compelling them to hide in mountain caves. Whatever meager grain they raised they hid well, burying it in pits under the earth or in empty winepresses so their enemies wouldn't find it.

At that time, a man named Gideon was threshing wheat one day in a hidden place. He suddenly had a vision of "an angel of the LORD" sitting under an oak tree. "The LORD is with you, mighty warrior," the angel said. Gideon found it hard to believe God was with him after all that had happened. Though he must have been shaking in his sandals, Gideon questioned the angel.

"The LORD turned to him and said, 'Go in the strength you have and save Israel out of Midian's hand. Am I not sending you?'"

Gideon thought, *How could a humble servant like me do such a mighty thing?* So he said, "Pardon me, my lord…but how can I save Israel? My clan is the weakest in Manasseh, and I am the least in my family" (Judges 6:15).

God answered, "I will be with you, and you will strike down all the Midianites, leaving none alive" (verse 16).

Gideon felt certain the angel was delivering God's words to him. So he left and brought back an offering of a young goat and unleavened bread and laid them on a rock before the heavenly messenger. The angel touched the offering with his staff. Immediately fire leaped up and consumed it. Then the angel disappeared. Gideon shook with fear when he saw what happened, but God reassured him. "Peace! Do not be afraid. You are not going to die."

Gideon seized the moment to build an altar under the oak tree near the village of Ophrah, in the tribal land of Manasseh where God appeared to him. He called it by a name that meant "The LORD Is Peace."

God instructed Gideon what to do next. Before liberating the Israelites from the Midianites, Gideon must set them free from Baal and Asherah worship, two false gods the people were following. God told Gideon to destroy the altar to Baal and tear down the Asherah pole his father had built.

That very night Gideon took 10 of his servants and destroyed the altar and threw down the image of Baal and cut the wooden pole of Asherah into pieces. In their place he built an altar to the God of Israel, using the broken pieces of the idols for wood and sacrificing a young ox as a burnt offering.

The following morning, when the villagers came out to worship their idols, they found an altar to the living God where the idols had once stood. They looked at the broken and burning idols and wondered who had done this. They carefully investigated and called for the death of the perpetrators!

One person came forward and said, "Gideon son of Joash did it." The group whispered among themselves and then marched straight to Gideon's father, Joash. With anger and outrage, they shouted,

"Bring out your son. He must die, because he has broken down Baal's altar and cut down the Asherah pole beside it" (Judges 6:30).

Joash shot back the perfect reply. "If Baal really is a god, he can defend himself when someone breaks down his altar."

But Baal had no power to punish Gideon, so when the people saw this they turned back to the one true God.

Gideon then sent messengers throughout his tribe and some of the others, summoning all the men to fight. They met beside a great spring on Mount Gilboa, called "the spring of Harod" (Judges 7:1). From there they could look down on the Midianite army. How frightened the men in Gideon's "army" must have felt, for they were armed only with pitchers with lamps inside them and trumpets. They were also greatly outnumbered by their enemies.

What a solemn time it must have been. Gideon recognized the severity of the situation, and he wanted to be certain that it was God who was leading him and not his own imagination. He prayed expectantly, "If you will save Israel by my hand as you have promised—look, I will place a wool fleece on the threshing floor. If there is dew only on the fleece and all the ground is dry, then I will know that you will save Israel by my hand, as you said" (Judges 6:36).

And that is what happened. Gideon rose early the next day and squeezed the fleece and wrung out the dew leaving a bowlful of water. But Gideon asked for even more proof. "Do not be angry with me. Let me make just one more request. Allow me one more test with the fleece, but this time make the fleece dry and let the ground be covered with dew" (verse 39). That night God did so. Only the fleece was dry. All around it, the grass and bushes and trees were covered with dew. Gideon was now sure God had called him and would give him victory over the enemies of Israel at just the right moment in his timing.

Only faith is sufficient.
Robert Ley

Tea and Cookies

Each of you should use whatever gift you have received to serve others, as faithful stewards of God's grace in its various forms.
1 Peter 4:10

Pat felt scared and excited at the thought of moving from her small, comfortable house to a larger home in a lovely new neighborhood. Her three children were growing, and she wanted a bedroom for each one. The kids liked that idea as well. But as she looked at the boxes piled up in each room, ready to be loaded into the moving van, she sat down and cried. She prayed to be happy once again. It was so hard to leave old friends, familiar surroundings, and the area where she'd shopped and lived for eight years.

"We'd planned this event for months," she said. "I knew the move was God's gift to us. We'd have a pretty yard overlooking a wild canyon, a big kitchen with modern appliances, and the perfect place to plant my favorite flowers." But that day as she sat at the kitchen table, nothing could console her. "I was grieving. I missed our old neighborhood already. The kids had been able to walk to school, and I could take my dog to the park just two blocks away. I wondered if I'd ever feel at home in a big house on a block where I didn't know another soul."

Pat and her family arrived at their new place on a Monday morning in mid summer. Everyone ran inside to check the layout once again, the kids shouting to each other as they dashed from room to room. "I looked out the kitchen window," Pat said while nursing a cup of tea. "I thought, 'Lord, help me get a grip,' and God seemed to take the words to heart right away."

Later that week, Pat noticed a woman about her age walking up the driveway to the front door. "Oh great," she mumbled. "Someone wants to sell me something. Well, I'm not buying! We don't even have the boxes unpacked." She dabbed her eyes with a tissue, tucked in her shirt, and answered the knock on the door.

"Hello!" the woman said, smiling. "I'm Jean Sanchez. I live in the yellow house at the end of the cul-de-sac. Welcome to our neighborhood! I would have come sooner, but I wanted to give you a few days to get settled." Then she handed Pat a lovely glass jar with a red bow on top. "I call this concoction 'friendship tea,'" she said. "It's a mixture of iced tea crystals and orange Tang. Add water and ice, stir and enjoy. And here's a dozen homemade cookies to go with it."

Tears welled in Pat's eyes again, but this time from gratitude. "Here was a gift so lovely, so unexpected, so like the Lord that I was speechless. God had answered my prayer for comfort and friendship in the nick of time. I knew then I'd be at home wherever I lived as long as he was with me."

Pat reached out and hugged Jean. Then she suggested they sit down right then and enjoy a glass of friendship tea together.

We do not remember days, we remember moments.
Cesare Pavese

If the Shoe Fits...

*Better one handful with tranquility than two handfuls
with toil and chasing after the wind.*
ECCLESIASTES 4:6

Lorna had been a debtor. She ran up charge cards and was always late paying her bills. "I was a sucker when it came to loaning money to friends and family and then letting things slide when they didn't repay me within a reasonable amount of time." On the other hand, she was frugal when it came to buying clothes or shoes for herself. "I also had a hard time holding onto a job. I moved from one company to another at least seven or eight times in a five-year period. It was awful."

Lorna heard from an acquaintance about a program for debtors based on the 12 steps of Alcoholics Anonymous. She began attending meetings, and gradually she became financially solvent. "I still slip up from time to time when I see someone in worse shape than I am. I feel sad so I hand over money I have no business giving away since I have my own bills to pay."

Today Lorna is more aware than she was years ago. She admits that her money-loaning action can actually be disrespectful toward others. "I'd do well to help people find jobs so they can rebuild their self-respect and take care of themselves," she said.

Lorna knows that sometimes a gift given in the right spirit can be a blessing. A few years ago when she was about to go for an interview for a sales job, she realized she had nothing suitable to wear. "I rummaged through my closet, and I'm embarrassed to say I had one black skirt that could pass and a couple of tops I could make do with. But I didn't have any appropriate footwear. Flip-flops and tennis shoes were all I had to my name. Neither would do for a job interview."

At the time, Lorna was nearly out of money. She refused to borrow from a friend or put the purchase on credit, fearing it would start the debt cycle all over again. Instead, she used the tools of her recovery program, "praying for the knowledge of God's will and the power to carry it out" without going into debt. Lorna sensed that God had brought this job opportunity into her life, so she knew he'd provide a way for her to get it, right down to the last detail of her wardrobe.

She began praying each day for a surprise. She didn't want to tell God what to do, rather she was going to wait and see what he would do. "Sometimes I felt foolish," she said. "I wondered if I were playing a game with God."

Days later her aunt called from a nearby town and asked if she could stop by the following week. Lorna welcomed the chance to talk with her Aunt Rose. The women got together and, while eating lunch, Lorna shared her excitement about the possibility of new employment. She decided *not* to mention her need for shoes because she didn't want to sound as if she were looking for a handout.

At the end of the visit Rose paused at the door. "I almost forgot. I don't want to insult you, but I have a pair of shoes I bought a while ago that simply don't fit me correctly. I never should have purchased them. But I did, and it's too late now to exchange them. I think we wear about the same size." She glanced at Lorna's tennis shoes. "Do you want to take a look?"

Lorna hurriedly grabbed a breath. She stuffed the laughter that felt like it was going to explode. "Sure, I'd be glad to," she said, trying to sound casual.

Rose hurried out to her car and returned with a pair of size ten, navy pumps that looked as good as new. Lorna slipped them on, and they fit perfectly. The heel was the right height, and the simple style was ideal for a business interview. Lorna glanced up and whispered a prayer of thanks to God for dropping a pair of shoes into her life in the nick of time. Then she turned to Aunt Rose and told her the whole story. The two women glanced heavenward with smiles and more words of thanks and praise.

*Never let a problem to be solved become more important
than a person to be loved.*

Barbara Johnson

Prayer Stop

Children's children are a crown to the aged.
PROVERBS 17:6

For nine months Jim Warren had waited for this moment. "I was going to be a great-grandpa for the first time." He shared that his granddaughter Shelsea lay in a hospital bed anticipating the birth of her first child, a son she planned to name Matthew. Jim's daughter and Shelsea's mom, Lisa, was in the hospital room, along with Lisa's new fiancé, and Shelsea's dad. The rest of the family, including Jim, sat in the waiting room, expecting the new dad to burst through the door at any moment, grinning from ear-to-ear with the news of the baby's arrival.

As Jim found out later, behind the closed doors of the labor room everything was going well. Shelsea followed the doctor's directions. "Push ...push...you're doing great," he encouraged. Then suddenly something went wrong. The baby's heart monitor indicated distress and a rapidly decreasing blood pressure.

"We need to do a C-section *now!*" the doctor exclaimed. "Get her unplugged!" Two people in scrubs burst into the room. In seconds they'd unhooked Shelsea from the baby monitor and hustled her out the door, hospital bed and all.

Lisa became frantic. "What's wrong?" she asked.

As they wheeled Shelsea down the hall, the doctor shouted back, "The baby is in distress."

Lisa remained in her chair emotionally and physically frozen.

The doctors had just taken her daughter away. What was once a room full of joy was now empty except for a jumble of disconnected wires haphazardly thrown on the floor. Lisa's fiancé ran to the waiting room to update the family. Everyone hurried to Room 4, where Shelsea's mother sat crying uncontrollably. "We all huddled together and prayed," said Jim. "As I prayed, I felt in my spirit that God would bring Shelsea and Matthew through to victory. I believed he was letting me know through the Holy Spirit that he had things under control but to keep praying the persistent prayer of Hannah. Remember, she's the one who was barren for so long."

Jim continued. "It seemed like hours had passed, but it was really only a matter of minutes when we received word that mother and baby were fine. The umbilical cord had wrapped around the infant's neck, and as soon as little Matthew was freed, he bounced back to good health." Jim got everyone's attention and prayed on the spot in thanksgiving for God's solution that came just in the nick of time. "Thank you, Jesus, for protecting my granddaughter. And thank you for saving my great-grandson from death's grip."

Today, no matter the severity of a situation, Jim has peace when he prays because he knows God is with him. "I've learned to forget the enemy's plan, to stop worrying about what my circumstances are, and, instead, to look at God's plan and his love for me. This incident with Shelsea and Matthew strengthened my confidence in my identity in Christ."

Problems are not stop signs, they are guidelines.
Robert H. Schuller

Under the Palm Tree

With God we will gain the victory,
and he will trample down our enemies.

PSALM 60:12

The people of Israel during the fourth century BC were gradually swayed by the idol-worshippers around them. They began praying to false gods and behaving in immoral ways. They knew better than to turn against the one true God, but they did it anyway. God let them suffer the consequences of their sins.

At that time, Jabin, the Canaanite king, saw his opportunity to conquer the Israelites. Under the command of his general, Sisera, the Canaanites used chariots fitted with iron and drawn by horses to quickly subdue the Israelites, who weren't used to that kind of warfare. All the tribes in the land of Israel fell to the harsh rule and power of the dictator. It was the fourth such oppression they'd experienced, and it weighed heavily on them. Some good came of this experience though. After 20 years, the suffering tribes turned away from their idols and called upon the one true God again.

During this time, an Israeli woman named Deborah, God's prophet and a wife, was leading Israel. She held court under a palm tree called "the Palm of Deborah," located north of Jerusalem between the cities of Ramah and Bethel. There she served God, dispensed his wisdom, settled disputes, and offered advice to anyone who sought her help.

She was considered so wise and good that people traveled from all parts of the land to bring her their dilemmas and ask questions about life. Deborah ruled by the Spirit of God upon her, not by military standards or by government appointment. When she heard of the troubles of the Israeli tribes in the north and the harsh authority of the Canaanites, she took action. Because she was a woman of God, it's likely she sought God's wisdom and guidance through much prayer. Deborah knew from whom she received her power and influence!

After hearing from the Lord, she sent an important message to a brave man named Barak, who lived in the land of Naphtali. "The LORD, the God of Israel, commands you: 'Go, take with you ten thousand men of Naphtali and Zebulun and lead them up to Mount Tabor. I will lead Sisera, the commander of Jabin's army, with his chariots and his troops to the Kishon River and give him into your hands'" (Judges 4:6-7).

Barak, however, was afraid to take on such a huge task. He replied to Deborah, "If you go with me, I will go; but if you don't go with me, I won't go."

"Certainly I will go with you," Deborah replied. "But because of the course you are taking, the honor will not be yours, for the LORD will deliver Sisera into the hands of a woman" (verse 9).

Can you imagine how Barak felt at that point? He had been considered a wise and brave warrior, but he caved at the thought of setting out against the mighty Sisera and the Canaanites—even though Deborah had said the command was from God.

His resistance didn't stop Deborah, however! She left her seat under the palm tree and went up to Kedesh, where Barak lived. She likely prayed during her entire journey, bathing the huge undertaking with petitions for wisdom and guidance and safety.

When she and her entourage arrived at Barak's home, Barak sent out a call for fighting men from Zebulun and Naphtali. Ten thousand men met together with whatever weapons they could find. This small army, with Barak and Deborah in the lead, encamped on Mount Tabor, the site of many great battles. A brook called Kishon winds through this plain, becoming a rushing, foaming river during seasons of heavy rainfall. From their camp on the top of Mount Tabor, Barak's army could look down on the great host of

Canaanites with their many tents, horses, and chariots, as well as their general, Sisera.

Deborah was not afraid. She must have prayed day and night, knowing that God would keep his promise if she kept hers—to obey his command. She told Barak, "Go! This is the day the LORD has given Sisera into your hands. Has not the LORD gone ahead of you?" (Judges 4:14).

Deborah knew the God she served, and she trusted him with all her heart and mind. Her commitment must have been contagious because Barak followed her orders. As was the custom, he probably blew a trumpet and called for his men to rush down the side of the mountain and overtake the enemy. They did so—and God was with them.

The Canaanites were so surprised some had no time to even mount their chariots. Terrified, they all tried to escape, trampling each other as chaos reigned. And the Lord helped the Israelites—in the nick of time, for at that very moment the brook of Kishon swelled into a river. Many Canaanites stampeded right into it and were swept away (Judges 5:21). The rest of the Canaanites were killed by the sword, except for Sisera. As Deborah had prophesied, Sisera was killed by a woman. Jael lured him into her tent and, while he was sleeping, drove a tent peg through his temple.

A bold onset is half the battle.

Giuseppe Garibaldi

George Mueller was a maverick in his spiritual life, believing that in everything God would provide. He never asked anyone for money for his ministries or himself. Instead, he prayed that God would move people to help. According to John Piper, Mueller's passion was to "live a life and lead a ministry in a way that proves God is real, God is trustworthy, God answers prayer." Here is an excerpt from Mueller's diary:

> January 31, 1846. It is now 89 days since I have been daily waiting upon God about the building of an Orphan House. The time seems to be now near when the Lord will give us a piece of ground, and I told the brethren and sisters so this evening, after our usual Saturday evening prayer meeting at the Orphan Houses.

Mueller then heard of a suitable piece of property and tried in vain to find the owner at two different times so he could discuss the matter with him. He even considered stopping by the man's home but then sensed God holding him back, possibly for a higher purpose. He decided to "let patience have her perfect work." On February 5, the man contacted Mueller, confessing that he awoke at three o'clock that morning, unable to get back to sleep until five, preoccupied with the piece of land and determining that if Mueller applied for it he would sell it to him at a great discount.

> The agreement was made that morning, and I purchased a field of nearly seven acres...Observe the hand of God in my not finding the owner at home last evening! The Lord meant to speak to his servant first about these matters during a sleepless night, and to lead him fully to decide, before I had seen him.

George Mueller, *Answers to Prayer*

Joy in the Mourning

This God is our God for ever and ever;
he will be our guide even to the end.
PSALM 48:14

"Karen, your dad has taken a downturn." This message from my husband was waiting for me when I checked into a hotel after a trip to the mountains. I sensed my father's end was near. He'd been suffering for a long time, and his decline over the past few months was apparent. I decided to go directly to the nursing home some six hours away.

I zipped down the freeway, preoccupied with thoughts of all the ups and downs our relationship had undergone over the years. I was filled with memories...of the time he and I sang a duet at a Girl Scout father/daughter dinner, of the time we rode horses together at a dude ranch in Arizona, of the time he wouldn't speak to me for six months because we had some fundamental disagreements about religion, of the time he and I prayed together for God's forgiveness, of the time he held his first grandchild and then his first great-grandchild with the same tenderness.

I arrived at the nursing home at one-thirty that afternoon. My sister June and her husband, Harry, rushed in a couple of hours later. We joined our mother at Dad's bedside. He had slipped into a coma and no longer squeezed my hand when I reached for his.

The head nurse entered the room and told us quietly that our father was in the final moments of his life. I could barely stand to watch my father struggle so. Each breath was labored. *Dear God, release him,* I prayed silently. *Please take him home soon. He has waited so long for the touch of your healing hand. I give him back to you, O Lord.*

Suddenly a passage from Scripture came to mind. Quickly, I flipped to the concordance in the back of my Bible. I found the key word that took me to Philippians 3:14. In that moment, I had a brand-new understanding of what was occurring in front of my eyes. I read the passage aloud: "I press on toward the goal to win the prize for which God has called me heavenward in Christ Jesus."

Dad, indeed, was pressing on toward the goal. He was in the final sprint of the race of his life. Of course he couldn't squeeze my hand. Of course he couldn't turn and acknowledge our presence. Of course he was preoccupied with what was happening to his body. And of course he was breathing hard and fast. That's what runners do, especially when they are coming down to the finish line. They press on toward that goal. This was a private moment between the Lord and my father, and I had the privilege of observing it. My somber mood began to lift. Small tendrils of peace—even bits of joy—crept to the surface. I couldn't explain it. My father was about to die, and I was feeling happy.

My sister and I kissed our mother and father goodnight at nine o'clock, intending to return at seven the next morning. Later that evening the phone rang. It was the nurse at the station outside Dad's room.

"Your father is gone," she said simply.

Reality. Finality. Dad had died. He had crossed the finish line, and now he was in full possession of the prize for which he had run so long and hard—the call of God from above. What a moment for us both.

Praise our God who comforts us in grief by turning our mourning into joy in the nick of time—so we can celebrate the gifts of life and death.

It is during our darkest moments that we must focus to see the light.
Aristotle Onassis

God's Car

Anyone who believes in [Jesus] will never be put to shame.
ROMANS 10:11

"In the autumn of 2010, my husband's business was failing," shared Charise. "I'd been laid off from my job, and we had a newborn. We'd exhausted our savings to cover the shortfall in my husband's income, and my severance pay was spent. Bottom line? We were stuck and rent was due."

Charise and Ken had two limited options and both were unpleasant. "We could give our notice to move so our security deposit would cover the last month of rent or we could borrow the money and go deeper in debt." The first of the month was just ahead. They had to act—and fast. They turned to a car they'd put up for sale the year before that hadn't sold. "It was a classic to some and a pile of junk to others," said Charise. "But it was one we'd loved—especially my husband, who's a car guy. He grieves the sale of an automobile the way some people grieve the death of a pet."

They knew selling it was the right thing do, and they'd had several discussions about who would be the perfect owner: "someone who would treasure the car and even have the funds to restore it." Now, as their need for money increased, the dream owner became anyone who could pay what they were asking.

As a last-ditch effort, Ken reposted the ad for the car. "We had less than a week before we had to speak to the landlord. Within 24 hours two offers came in, one from out of the area. He was second in line, but his offer was for more money than the first one." When the first prospect heard this, he topped the offer and said he'd come to the house the following morning with cash in hand. He looked at the car, and then proceeded to have a lengthy phone call with a Mercedes specialist in Germany.

"We were more nervous by the minute," said Charise. "Then suddenly he turned to Ken and handed over the money. He said he was thrilled with the car and would return to pick it up in two days."

The couple was grateful to receive the cash they needed *and* that the car was being purchased by someone who was going to ship it back to Germany—its original home—for a full restoration. "We were able to cover our rent *and* get our dream owner in the nick of time," said Charise. "To top it off, the buyer's name was Christian."

She admitted they hadn't prayed about getting the rent money or selling the car. However, they did pray about their finances in general, asking God to lead them in determining if Ken should close the doors on his fledgling business and, if so, when. "We also wanted to know if I should go back to work, even though that meant leaving our infant in childcare sooner than we'd planned."

Sometimes Charise just cried and let her tears be her prayer, "knowing the Holy Spirit would translate my worry and fears into words. Desperation does create persistence in prayer," she added. "I learned that God has answers I can't imagine. He doesn't mess around. He works purposefully.

"This whole thing unfolded so far beyond what we could imagine, down to the smallest detail (the buyer's name!), that it took my breath away. I felt like how the disciples on the ship must have when Jesus stopped the wind. I was awestruck. I was humbled. I was convinced. I have faced a few more rough seas since that month, and I have truly been able to embrace God's peace and rest, knowing he will always provide.

"When peace is threatened, I often picture that cute little blue car heading home to Germany on a big ship and a guy named Christian God used to allow our family to stay in our home," Charise said.

When you reach the end of your rope, tie a knot in it and hang on.
Thomas Jefferson

Cottage on the River

*Trust in the LORD with all your heart and lean not
on your own understanding; in all your ways
submit to him, and he will make your paths straight.*
PROVERBS 3:5-6

Bev and her first husband, Mac, built a large, brick house in North East, Maryland, for their growing family. One day after their son graduated from high school, they were attracted to the waterfront homes in Cecil County, especially one sweet cottage with a deck that extended down to the beach on the banks of the Bohemia River. They fell in love with the place and the spectacular view, even though the home was two sizes smaller than the one they were living in.

"We came up with a small down payment and an agreement to purchase based on the contingency of selling our brick house," said Bev. "We obtained a 'bridge loan' to make payments each month to the Realtor, who would consider us the buyers for at least one year." After that period, if the family couldn't make the final purchase price, the Realtor would be free to offer it to another party. Bev and her husband put the family home up for sale and waited prayerfully for someone to buy it.

Ten months passed without a sale. They were no closer to moving to the cottage by the river than they were when they made the down payment. "At one point, I prayed and fasted for three days asking God to bring a buyer," added Bev. "Real estate was in high demand, so we couldn't understand why no one wanted our beautiful house. During that time I spent many hours on my knees asking God for his will in the sale. My husband had invested most of the physical energy into building it, while I'd contributed most of the prayer energy."

Bev wanted God to bring "a buyer who would love and take care of the house and upgrade the windows, landscaping, and basement." But God appeared to be ignoring their prayers. They began doubting their decision to sell. Time after time they jumped into their car and drove to the cottage to visit the patient owners. "We always left assured we were doing the right thing, but still no buyer for our family home appeared," Bev said.

Sometimes Bev cried in frustration and anxiety, depressed over what appeared to be a lack of attention from God when they were so anxious for an answer. She could see the tension in her husband, and she knew how much he needed to have this burden lifted from his shoulders. Bev admitted she'd acted like a child when she didn't get her way. "I learned I was completely self-centered in the way I prayed." She stopped going to church because she was so upset about the uncertainty of both transactions. "In addition, my husband and I were in a funk in our marriage. We'd hoped this change of home location might energize us again."

Then just one month before the end of the contract regarding the cottage, God brought the right buyers! "At last we were able to move into the cottage and enjoy swimming and boating in the river. But, more important, it was there my relationship with God changed," said Bev. "My husband and I divorced three years later, and I realized at that time that I needed the calm and beauty of this location to work through the grief I felt over my marriage ending and to rebuild my self-esteem."

God was more than present with Bev during that time. Through Scripture and time spent with her, God showed Bev she was his and he loved her and would be with her forever. When fear and painful memories sprang up, the Lord renewed her mind. "I learned that he is the blessed controller of all things," she said. "He is my husband,

my protector, and my provider, and will be until the end of my life.
I am a daughter of the King and no longer afraid."

Keep your fears to yourself, but share your courage with others.

Robert Louis Stevenson

The Phone Call

*Do not be anxious about anything, but in every situation,
by prayer and petition, with thanksgiving,
present your requests to God.*

PHILIPPIANS 4:6

In 2003, Judy Durden noticed burning and numbness in her hands. "I couldn't do simple things such as open a door, unscrew a bottle cap, use a can opener, or hold a container of shampoo to wash my hair. Soon the pain spread to all my limbs," she said. Even getting up from a chair became a challenge. She started waking up in the middle of the night with fire-like pain in her hands, and then she couldn't get back to sleep. Judy followed up with her doctor and then a surgeon who recommended tests for carpal tunnel syndrome. However, there was a four-month-long waiting list for this treatment. Judy wondered how she could hold on that long. "I was at the point where I couldn't even bathe myself. I remember being in the shower, tears streaming down my face, and asking God to help me. I was losing the ability to do even basic things."

The surgeon made a phone call to see if he could shorten the waiting time, but he was told many others were on the list too. In addition to that, it would take five months before Judy could be scheduled to have the necessary surgery.

"My husband and I prayed very hard for an opening. One afternoon, feeling totally discouraged while leaving the surgeon's office, Dennis and I heard the phone ring at the nurse's station. A nurse answered and then called out my name. The call was from the specialist saying that if I could arrive at his office by five o'clock the next afternoon, he would administer the necessary electrical current test."

Relief and gratitude flooded Judy's mind and heart. "God *does* answer prayer!" she whispered.

The following day the couple arrived at the specialist's office. Judy was nervous because she didn't know what to expect. "Let me just say it wasn't fun when the doctor stuck little pins down my arms and legs and then shocked me with electrical current." The percentage of pain registered was enough to qualify Judy for carpal tunnel surgery on her hands. "I can't begin to say how thankful I was to be able to receive the treatment I needed. From there I met with a rheumatologist who, after examining me, told me I had an autoimmune disease called rheumatoid arthritis (RA), for which there is no cure. The disease had struck my wrists first, and that's what started the carpal tunnel pain."

Judy underwent surgery on both hands, and the physician placed her on chemotherapy weekly, which is used for RA as well as lupus and cancer. She takes six methotrexate pills every Monday and prednisone twice a day. "I prefer the pills to injections," said Judy. "I am so grateful for this medication that keeps me from being crippled. As a contractor in the construction trade, I'm now able to do all the things I could do before I was diagnosed."

Judy admits she still struggles with her condition daily, but without the medicine and treatment she wouldn't be able to carry on. "I thank God for all he has given me. There were many times when I felt sure I'd never get through this. Time passed so slowly and the pain never ceased. I often felt overwhelmed."

During that time, Judy and Dennis persisted in prayer. "We spent a lot of time on our knees, asking God for strength to pull through this experience. I prayed that he would make me a stronger person and give me patience."

Today Judy's faith is deeper than ever. "The book of Hebrews talks about trusting in things you can't see. It's so easy to believe that when life is going well. It's harder when things are difficult. My relationship with God has deepened dramatically," she said. "I don't worry as much as I once did. I know now that no matter how bad things get, I am never alone. God is always at my side and on my side. I pray a lot more now as well, in good times and in bad times. Pastor Charles Stanley said something that I will never forget. 'A storm is inevitable, an anchor is unmovable.'"

Wherever you are, be all there.
Jim Elliot

The Great Test

*No good thing does [the LORD] withhold
from those whose walk is blameless.*
PSALM 84:11

About 521 BC, King Darius, ruling over the empire of Persia, gave a place of honor and power to Daniel, one of God's prophets. Daniel was a very old man at the time. The king saw that Daniel, above all the others, was wise in every way.

This recognition, however, didn't go over well with the other rulers and princes. They were jealous and eager to discredit Daniel, to find something evil about him so they could report it to the king. They began paying attention to his every action. One thing they did know about him was that three times each day he went to his room, opened the window that faced Jerusalem, and prayed to God. Although Jerusalem was in ruins and the Jewish temple was no longer standing, Daniel continued this ritual of gazing toward the place where the house of God once stood, even though it was hundreds of miles away.

The jealous noblemen agreed that it would not be easy to pin something on him. "We will never find any basis for charges against this man Daniel unless it has something to do with the law of his God" (Daniel 6:5). But they were unwilling to give up. They decided to plot against him by approaching the king with a proposal to change Persian law.

"The royal administrators, prefects, satraps, advisers and gover-
nors have all agreed that the king should issue an edict and enforce
the decree that anyone who prays to any god or human being during the next thirty days, except to you, Your Majesty, shall be thrown
into the lions' den" (verse 7). Then they pressed for this plan to be
made into law. "Now, Your Majesty, issue the decree and put it in
writing so that it cannot be altered—in accordance with the law of
the Medes and Persians, which cannot be repealed." King Darius
followed their suggestions and put the decree in writing.

Although the edict went out, Daniel continued praying three
times a day. He might have been scared. He might have wondered
if his life would be spared. Maybe he even pleaded with God to safe-
guard him. We do know that he kept on praying, trusting God for
his life (verse 10).

This infuriated the men who spied on him. So they returned to
the king and reminded him about his new law. "Did you not publish a decree that during the next thirty days anyone who prays to
any god or human being except to you, Your Majesty, would be
thrown into the lions' den?"

The king answered that he had.

Then the nobles took great delight in betraying Daniel. Daniel
still prays three times a day, they reported to the king. Can't you just
imagine their haughty attitude and feeling of certainty that they'd
trapped God's prophet once and for all?

Upon hearing this news, the king was greatly troubled. He considered Daniel a friend as well as a trustworthy ruler. With great
reluctance, King Darius issued the order that Daniel be thrown
into the lions' den. "May your God, whom you serve continually,
rescue you!" he declared as servants tossed the old man into the pit
and sealed the opening with a large stone. Then the king returned
to his palace and spent the night without food or entertainment or
sleep, perhaps praying through till dawn, when he left his bedcham-
ber and hurried to the lions' den. He called to Daniel, "Daniel, servant of the living God, has your God, whom you serve continually,
been able to rescue you from the lions?"

Daniel was quick to answer, for the God he loved and served had saved his life in the nick of time despite the hungry lions prowling around him. "May the king live forever! My God sent his angel, and he shut the mouths of the lions. They have not hurt me, because I was found innocent in his sight. Nor have I ever done any wrong before you, Your Majesty."

The king was jubilant! He ordered his servants to lift Daniel out of the den. He was surprised that not even a scratch marred Daniel's body because he'd trusted God.

The men who had deceived the king and accused Daniel were brought in, and the king ordered them thrown into the lions' den, along with their wives and children. Before they even reached the floor, the lions attacked and killed them.

Then King Darius wrote to all the nations and peoples of the earth. "I issue a decree that in every part of my kingdom people must fear and reverence the God of Daniel."

Perseverance, secret of all triumphs.
Victor Hugo

Wanted: Your Book

God is able to bless you abundantly, so that in all things
at all times, having all that you need,
you will abound in every good work.
2 CORINTHIANS 9:8

"From the time I was a child, I longed to write a novel," Joe Bentz shared. "I felt writing was a calling from the Lord, and I pursued it more than any other interest. I started out as a journalism major in college and then switched to English. Through my college years, including graduate school, I continued writing fiction in addition to the academic work required."

An idea for a fantasy novel began forming in Joe's mind. It took close to ten years to complete the story. "These were years when I was busy with other pursuits as well, including starting my teaching career. I didn't write as consistently as I should have, but I kept coming back to the book. Eventually, it grew to a gargantuan 1200 pages! Then I revised it and whittled it down to about half that length. One day I wrote a book proposal and sent it out to a variety of publishers and followed up with fervent prayers."

Joe admits that he was naïve about the publishing world. "I didn't have any idea how difficult it was to publish a novel, especially Christian fantasy. I had never studied the business side of writing because I wanted to focus my attention on writing a good book. I figured there would be plenty of time later on to bend to publishers's demands…if I had to."

The rejections came swiftly. "I was appalled that some editors returned my proposal without even opening the envelope. This was my life's work, and they couldn't be bothered to even glance at it? Eventually two asked to see the full manuscript, so I still had hope. Then one of them rejected it."

The second editor read the manuscript and loved it. Joe thought his dream of publishing a book was about to come true. However, he didn't know at the time about publication committees, and how each member has to sign off on a book before a contract can be offered. "When I heard about this protocol, I assumed this was simply a formality so I didn't worry about it."

The publishing committee said no. They rejected the book several months after the editor had raved about it. "My disappointment was even greater than if they had simply rejected the book to begin with. I was crushed. I felt as if God had answered my prayer and then took it back."

Generally, when a publication committee vetoes a proposal, that's the end of it. The author moves on to another company or project. "But the editor said he believed in the book so strongly that he wanted me to make some revisions, and then he would take it back to the naysayers for another chance. There were no guarantees this would work, but he asked if I'd be willing to give it a go. I agreed," Joe said.

He spent the next several months rewriting, and then he submitted the new version. "The editor took the book back to the committee, and a few months later—a full year after I had submitted the original proposal—the publisher offered a contract. My first novel, *Song of Fire*, was published by Thomas Nelson the next year."

Joe learned that the "end" of an experience is not necessarily a finality. "God's ways are mysterious, to say the least. And his timing is not my timing. Trusting in him can be as nerve-wracking as watching a suspense thriller. But I believe he redeems the work I have put in, even if in a different way than I anticipate," said Joe. "I am learning not to take shortcuts, not to force my way, and not to give in to despair when things don't turn out the way I think they should. I don't have the full perspective that I will have even a few years from now, let alone through eternity. I choose to trust God even when he doesn't respond until the nick of time."

Do not anticipate trouble, or worry about what may never happen.
Keep in the sunlight.
Benjamin Franklin

Our Heavenly Father is the husbandman. He understands the rough stock of our humanity. He know its evil nature and its little worth, but he also knows how to put within it a new nature. Not of our struggling or strife does it come, for it is not from within that this grace must spring, but by our surrender to the divine Gardener—letting him have his way perfectly with us in everything. If we will but permit him to put into us what he desires, he can get out of us what he wills. Receiving is more than asking; it is claiming and taking. The manifestation of his indwelling may be as gradual as the development of the bud in the briar, but be assured that it will be there.

Mrs. Charles E. Cowman,
Streams in the Desert 2

Two-by-Two

Carefully follow the terms of this covenant,
so that you may prosper in everything you do.
DEUTERONOMY 29:9

God was generous with Adam and Eve despite their sin of eating the forbidden fruit from the one tree in the Garden of Eden he'd declared off limits. He gave them long lives and blessed them with many children. By the time Adam died, the earth was filled with people—sons and daughters of Adam and Eve, their children, their children's children, and on through the generations.

Many, however, grew up and lived in sinful ways until there was so much wickedness in the world God decided to put a stop to it. "I will wipe from the face of the earth the human race I have created—and with them the animals, the birds and the creatures that move along the ground—for I regret that I have made them" (Genesis 6:7).

But even then God saw one good man. Noah was a righteous man, and he walked faithfully with God. As Noah walked and talked with him, the Lord said to him, "I am going to put an end to all people, for the earth is filled with violence because of them. I am surely going to destroy both them and the earth."

Imagine how Noah must have felt! Scared? Worried? At least momentarily. He listened carefully as God told him what to do. Then God said, "I will establish my covenant with you." What had Noah done to deserve such mercy? He certainly wasn't perfect. No human being is. I'm sure Noah was relieved to learn he'd found favor with God.

God told Noah to build a huge boat, an ark. It was to be very long and wide and deep—three stories high with a roof on top. Then he said:

> Go into the ark, you and your whole family, because I have found you righteous in this generation. Take with you seven pairs of every kind of clean animal, a male and its mate, and one pair of every kind of unclean animal, a male and its mate, and also seven pairs of every kind of bird, male and female, to keep their various kinds alive through- out the earth. Seven days from now I will send rain on the earth for forty days and forty nights, and I will wipe from the face of the earth every living creature I have made (Gen- esis 7:1-4).

Noah followed God's instructions exactly, though it must have appeared odd to everyone because there were no large bodies of water close by. But that didn't stop Noah, and perhaps his sons, from working on the great ship for many years. When they finished, it looked like a huge house on a dry piece of land. It had a door on one side and openings around the roofline to let in light and fresh air (Genesis 7:15-16).

Noah and his wife and sons and their families went into the ark, as God had instructed, taking with them the animals and birds, along with food for each kind. After every allowed human being and furry and feathered creatures were in place, the door of the ark was shut. No other people or animals could come aboard.

The heavens opened up and rain fell. Streams filled, and the riv- ers rose higher and higher. Soon the ark was afloat on the water. Men and women outside the ark panicked. They left their homes and ran up the mountains, but soon they were covered too, and every liv- ing land creature outside the ark drowned. For forty days and nights rain pounded the earth until there was not a breath of life on land anywhere outside the ark.

When the season came to an end, the rains ceased as quickly as they'd come. But the water flooded the earth for 150 days (Genesis 7:24). Those inside the ark stayed put, floating over the great sea until God sent a wind to blow across the waters and dry them up, little by little. Gradually, the mountains poked above the sea. Then the hills appeared. Finally the ark stopped floating and landed on "the mountains of Ararat."

Noah could not yet see what had happened because the door was shut and the only window was in the roof. But he could feel the ark was no longer floating. He waited for a time and then opened the window and let out a raven. It kept flying back and forth over the water. Noah eventually sent out a dove. The bird couldn't find a place to land, so it came back to the ark and Noah let it in. He waited another week and sent the dove out once more. That evening the dove came back to the ark holding in its bill a fresh leaf from an olive tree, a sure sign the water had gone down enough for trees to begin growing again.

Noah waited yet another week and sent the dove out but it did not return, meaning it probably found a place to roost. Maybe that meant it was safe for Noah and his family to disembark. He took off part of the roof and looked out. Dry land surrounded the ark. What a relief after a year with only his family and a slew of smelly animals to relate to. It doesn't take much to picture tempers rising while people and animals were so closely confined. Family members probably lost sleep with worry, and mealtimes became monotonous. The men and women surely wondered how all this would end, and when it did what they could look forward to. They'd have to start their lives from scratch.

God spoke to Noah and reassured him. "Come out of the ark, you and your wife and your sons and their wives. Bring out every kind of living creature that is with you—the birds, the animals, and all the creatures that move along the ground—so they can multiply on the earth and be fruitful and increase in number on it" (Genesis 8:16-17).

Noah opened the door of the ark, stepped out with his wife and sons and their wives, and stood once more on dry ground, probably taking great gulps of fresh, pure air. The first thing Noah did when his feet hit the land was to praise and thank God for saving him and his family. Perhaps they even sang and danced with joy! The animals and birds and creeping things filed out of the ark too, and the land was filled with life once more. Noah built an altar and laid upon it an offering to the Lord.

Pleased with Noah's offering, God said,

> Never again will I curse the ground because of humans, even though every inclination of the human heart is evil from childhood. And never again will I destroy all living creatures, as I have done. As long as the earth endures, seed-time and harvest, cold and heat, summer and winter, day and night will never cease (Genesis 8:21-22).

Just when the family might have wavered in their faith, wondering if they'd have to go through such an ordeal again, God came through in the nick of time—answering questions and concerns and earnest prayers. He splashed color across the heavens for all time and for all mankind. He caused this rainbow to appear in the sky and said,

> This is the sign of the covenant I am making between me and you and every living creature with you, a covenant for all generations to come: I have set my rainbow in the clouds, and it will be the sign of the covenant between me and the earth. Whenever I bring clouds over the earth and the rainbow appears in the clouds, I will remember my covenant between me and you and all living creatures of every kind (verses 12-15).

Obedience without faith is possible, but not faith without obedience.

Author unknown

The Father's Hand

You have been my hope, Sovereign LORD,
my confidence since my youth.
PSALM 71:5

Glenda and her family had just come home from an outing that included dinner and a short trip to the grocery store. "I recall going into the kitchen to put a few items into the refrigerator," she said, "but I noticed right away that my son Brian, 18 months old at the time, wasn't with me." She called his name, but when he didn't answer she rushed to the sliding door that overlooked the swimming pool. Relief swept over her when she realized the childproof lock on the fence was still in place.

A moment later she found her son in the living room holding up to his lips a glass cylinder that contained clear lamp oil. "As I screamed and ran to take it away from him, I realized I was seconds too late. He drank some of the liquid and a little even dribbled down his chin. I bundled him up and shouted for my husband, Cliff. We called Poison Control and were told to take Brian to the hospital immediately."

As Cliff drove, Brian was turning blue. When they arrived at the hospital, the emergency personnel took him from Glenda's arms and pumped his stomach.

"The most pressing memory I have of that time," said Glenda, "is praying over and over that the Lord would let him live and restore him to full health."

After Brian was stabilized, he was admitted to the pediatric unit. "Cliff and I took turns standing over his crib throughout the night. The next morning his doctor told us he'd passed the crisis point, and we could take him home. After a night of little to no sleep, we were exhausted. We made it home full of praise for answered prayer, ate a small lunch, and put Brian down for his nap."

Two hours later he awoke crying and feverish. "I scooped him up from his crib, and we raced back to the hospital," Glenda said. "We called family and friends to help care for our other children. Both sets of grandparents took turns sitting with Brian at the hospital during the day so Cliff and I could go to work. Everyone was praying for a miracle healing."

Brian's temperature climbed to 106 degrees and stayed there. He had apparently aspirated some of the lamp oil into his lungs and developed pneumonia. "With a fever and an unusually fast heart rate, Brian had to endure ice baths, daily X-rays of his chest, and different courses of antibiotics. However, the fever didn't break. Next he underwent a surgical procedure to extract fluid from his lungs so the technicians could take a culture." When he still didn't improve, he was transferred to Children's Hospital for further assessment. "Another week went by with no improvement," said Glenda, "so he returned to the primary hospital. As the days dragged on, the tiny arteries in his arms used for inserting IV fluids collapsed."

The doctor installed a main-line portal into his upper chest to keep the IV fluids moving into his small body. At the end of three weeks, the high fever continued, his breathing was labored, and large pockets of fluid still remained in his lungs. The only treatment option at that point was a procedure that involved placing a drain into his lung through the chest wall, requiring that he stay in the hospital for another four weeks.

"We were devastated by this news," Glenda shared. "All we could do was kiss Brian goodbye as the anesthetic took hold and surrender him into the hands of Jesus and the surgical team." While waiting for their son to recover from the surgery, Brian's parents headed to a nearby laundry to wash his favorite bear and blanket, now soiled with tears, IV fluids, and saliva. They grabbed a quick bite to eat before heading back to the recovery area waiting room. They checked in and received the news that the surgeon wanted to speak to them right away.

"As he came down the hallway toward us, Cliff and I feared the worst," Glenda said. "Did our little boy's heart just give out? Did he die on the operating table? My heart pounded. I couldn't bear to hear what the doctor had to tell us."

The doctor gave them "a very strange and wonderful report," Glenda said. "Every pocket of fluid in Brian's lungs had mysteriously disappeared!" The surgeon used a CT scan to assist him in inserting the drain tube and that was when he saw that all of the extra fluid was gone. He had no explanation for how this could have occurred.

Later, Cliff and Glenda learned that the plea for prayers for their son had reached across the ocean from San Diego to a prayer group in the Philippines. "To this day we will always be grateful for the thousands of believers who brought our son's plight before the throne of God in prayer."

Looking back, Brian's hospitalization changed the lives of their entire family and perhaps those of many doctors and nurses who worked with Brian and his parents. "I know that my walk with the Lord was strengthened and my prayer life deepened," said Glenda. "The term 'pray without ceasing' took on new meaning for Cliff and me and for all those who prayed for our son."

The Bible verse Glenda clung to at that time reminded her that "the temptations in your life are no different from what others experience. And God is faithful. He will not allow the temptation to be more than you can stand. When you are tempted, he will show you a way out so that you can endure" (1 Corinthians 10:13 NLT).

Glenda knew a miracle had occurred, and the final X-ray on the last day confirmed it. Recently, on a trip to the hospital pharmacy, Glenda said she ran into Brian's former pediatrician. "He told me the doctors and nurses who attended Brian talked about his healing long after the fact."

To this day their son is healthy and full of life at age 21. He has no breathing issues or lung problems. "In the nick of time and with 'groanings too deep for words,' the Holy Spirit lifted our son onto the lap of his heavenly Father, and he was healed" (Romans 8:26 NASB).

If you are going through hell, keep going.
Winston Churchill

Cross-Country Move

Put your outdoor work in order and get your fields ready;
after that, build your house.
PROVERBS 24:27

"I'll never forget how God came through for us at the last minute," Mike shared. "I'd accepted a new job that required a cross-country move. My wife, Deb, stayed behind to sell the house and wrap up various details." The couple hoped they'd only be separated for a month. Just then, however, the housing market tanked and their month extended to two and then three. "We felt assured that our move was God's plan and that he didn't want us to face both a mortgage payment and rent."

Their goal was to be settled in the new location together by Christmas of that year. Real estate traffic was next to nothing on their house, and people who did express interest made unrealistic offers, probably hoping to catch a deal from a desperate seller, Mike surmised.

Mike and Deb prayed for a buyer and also enlisted the prayers of friends, family, coworkers, and people in their new church. "We asked that we'd remain in God's will and not jump at wrong offers on the house. And if God didn't want us to sell it right then, that we'd find the right renter.

"We really needed the house sold, and we wanted to make some money on it," Mike said. "The Lord brought the ideal buyers at a price we could live with. Now we are trusting him to help us find a house in Colorado. In the meantime, we have an apartment that is more than adequate."

Mike said that most of the time he felt completely confident that God would provide. "The circumstances that brought me to my new job were so clearly God-ordained that I knew he would do what needed to be done. At times I felt impatient as I waited for Deb to join me, but I never doubted that we'd receive a solution from God."

Today, God is more real to Mike than ever before. He's now willing to step out in faith in other areas too. Learning and practicing patience continues. The couple is still waiting for the right job for Deb. "It's taking longer than we'd like," said Mike. "In the meantime, she can use this period to complete work on her master's degree and to share her teaching and administrative gifts at the church we've joined.

"God is providing for our needs on one income," he added, a challenge the couple has never faced before. They thank and praise him even as they wait and trust for what he'll provide next.

A journey may be long or short,
but it must start at the very spot one finds oneself.
Jim Stovall

The Red Bow

I have come that they may have life, and have it to the full.
JOHN 10:10

From the time I was in third grade I've wanted to be a writer of children's books. I loved books—the feel of them, the smell of them, and the looks of them. Trips to the library became my favorite outing as a child. It was a place of refuge. No one scolded me there. No one told me to sit up straight, drink my milk, or kiss a maiden aunt who had a mole on her face that scared me.

At the library people smiled. The lady behind the desk helped me find books just right for me. After checking them out, I remember skipping down the steps of the old building. I was the little girl with long brown hair, a big red bow, and an armload of books.

In high school I cut my hair and did away with bows. I was a young woman now. Life as a teenager wasn't a happy experience. I was small, physically immature, painfully shy, and obsessed with trying to belong.

I graduated and went off to college the following September. Life in a women's dorm was an adventure. I met new friends and felt growing confidence as I discovered that I could live away from home and make it. Something else happened that first year. Something wonderful but quite unexpected. I walked into the campus library, and a warm and familiar feeling came over me. I felt once again like the little girl with long brown hair and a big red bow who was safe within the boundaries of a library. I returned there every day to study, to read, and sometimes just to walk among the books—to look at them, to smell them, to touch them.

I graduated from college and got married two weeks later. I left behind the little girl with the big red bow. I didn't need her anymore. At last I belonged. I was somebody's wife and then a mother. I did grown-up things like sewing, cooking, needlepoint, and playing tennis with the ladies. I also taught Sunday school. For a while I was a teacher, and then I started a tutoring business in our home.

Children and children's books became important again as I introduced my son and two daughters to reading and weekly visits to the library. Sometimes I tied up my daughters' long hair with big red bows. And sometimes, with an armload of favorite books, we skipped down the library steps together.

All that changed when I went into counseling over my broken marriage. I stopped going to the library. I stopped going to church. I gave away my sewing machine, threw away my yarn and needles, and sold my tennis racket. I moved to San Diego.

Finally I felt hopeful. Maybe life could be good. I remarried in 1983. I returned to church. I discovered the mountains and the beaches. I found the library again! I forgot the pain. I also forgot the little girl with the big red bow.

But the pain came back. This time it wouldn't go away. Not in church. Not in prayer. Not in the mountains. Not in the library. Not at my typewriter. I entered private counseling with a new therapist in a new city to begin the hard work of rebuilding my inner life. It became the journey of a lifetime that included deep pain as I examined my childhood scars and began recovering. Then one day, after six years, my counselor and I agreed we were nearing the end of our work together. It would soon be time to say goodbye. We recounted some of my victories and listed the things I had overcome and let go of. Then a most unexpected thing occurred. I was overcome with weeping. Deep, racking sobs took my breath away. I couldn't even talk through the tears. *Where is this coming from?* I wondered.

My counselor encouraged me to close my eyes and let the feelings register. I did. And there in front of my mind was a picture so clear that it could have been hanging on the wall. I saw myself as a child in third grade, a joyful little girl with long brown hair and a big red bow, jumping up and down for all she was worth, and shouting at the top of her voice, "You found me! You found me! I've waited so long."

Oh dear God, I thought, sobbing again, *it's me!* The mental image perfectly matched a picture of myself at that age hanging in my bedroom.

I closed my eyes once more and there she was. But this time she was sitting on the floor in front of me, her head in my lap, her arms curled around my legs. Then she looked up and said in a voice I will never forget, "You don't have to cry anymore. We found each other, and we'll never be separated again." What joy! What freedom! I had found myself. At last I truly belonged.

I believe that child within is the keeper of the key. I'm convinced that all the therapy, books, recordings, seminars, and sermons would have been of no lasting help without my meeting and embracing that child only God could set me free to be.

So if you see me on the street, or in church, or at the supermarket, at a conference, or in the library, you may recognize me on the outside as an older woman with white hair and grandchildren. But don't let appearances fool you. I am really a little girl with long brown hair and a big red bow—the one God released in the nick of time.

You gain strength, courage, and confidence by every experience in which you really stop to look fear in the face.

Eleanor Roosevelt

Farewell, My Son

The LORD bestows favor and honor; no good thing does he
withhold from those whose walk is blameless.
PSALM 84:11

Pharaoh feared the increasing number of Jews in Egypt. They'd been a formidable presence in his country for 400 years. He pictured the men joining a foreign army and starting a rebellion against him and his people, so he ordered the killing of all male Hebrew babies (Exodus 1:16).

Jochebed, a young mother, gave birth to a beautiful and healthy boy. When she heard Pharaoh's order, she must have been shaken to the core. How unthinkable that her son would be murdered. Regardless of the Pharaoh's command, she hid her son for three months. But when he became too big to hide, she came up with a plan—one that would take enormous faith and courage to pull off. It might even mean she would never lay eyes on her child again. But she had to act quickly or he would be found and slaughtered.

She took advantage of a moment to herself by taking a papyrus basket and coating the bottom with tar and pitch to make it waterproof. Then she wrapped her baby in cloths, placed him inside the basket, and set it among the reeds on the bank of the Nile River. The child's older sister, Miriam, stood nearby to see what would happen to her brother.

All Jochebed's hopes and dreams of raising a strong son must have sailed away that day. Although Jochebed was a woman of great faith, I picture her weeping and praying that someone would find the child and raise him to be a man of God. She probably smothered her sweet one with kisses and strokes of love before surrendering him to the water, trusting God to do for him what she could not.

Pharaoh's daughter went to the river to bathe at that very hour. She saw the basket among the reeds and told one of her maidservants to bring it to her. When she opened it, there lay a baby crying and fussing. She felt sorry for him. "This is one of the Hebrew babies," she said.

Miriam saw Pharaoh's daughter holding her brother. She spoke up. "Shall I go and get one of the Hebrew women to nurse the baby for you?"

"Yes, go," she answered.

Miriam, of course, sought out her mother and returned with her to the noble woman. When they arrived, Pharaoh's daughter said to Jochebed, "Take this baby and nurse him for me, and I will pay you" (Exodus 2:9).

So the child's natural mother took him and nursed him while he grew. What an answer to prayer! Just when Jochebed had nearly given up hope that she would ever see the boy again, God provided the solution. When the boy grew older, Jochebed gave him back to Pharaoh's daughter. She named him Moses and raised him as her own.

Jochebed's trust in God was her greatest legacy to her children. She replaced her own feelings and fears with faith, believing God would care for her son. The Lord went above and beyond her expectations. He gave her the opportunity to nurse the baby and to care for him all the days of his early years. Little did Jochebed know she was playing a vital role in the making of the boy's future. Moses would one day lead the Hebrew people out of slavery and into the Promised Land God had set aside for them!

A wise unselfishness is not a surrender of yourself to the wishes of anyone, but only to the best discoverable course of action.

David Seabury

Praying Wife

All things are possible with God.
MARK 10:27

"Lord, *please* change Dan," Tami prayed—not once but many times during her 12-year marriage. She admits she was afraid her husband was slipping away from God. His life was filled with stress as he worked full time, attended graduate school, and carried the full financial burden for their family.

Tami begged, argued, cajoled, cried, and flat-out told Dan he should spend more time praying and studying his Bible, especially during that stressful season. She even strategically placed a Bible at the foot of their bed as a hint. "I tried everything I could think of to get him to change," said Tami. "I played mother, counselor, spiritual advisor—and even Holy Spirit," she added, smiling through her embarrassment as she recalled her controlling behavior.

Then one day after another episode in which she watched her husband choose again not to seek God's wisdom and help in a stressful situation, Tami became desperate and fed up. She stretched out on her living room floor, facedown, and prayed like she'd never prayed before.

"God," she cried, "Dan is yours! Please take charge of his life because I can't do it anymore." And something wonderful happened in that moment. "I felt the burden of my husband's relationship with God release from my grip. I knew God would answer my prayer." As Tami lay on the floor, she felt the Lord present her with

an idea. Instead of pestering Dan about getting spiritually in sync
with God, she could get together with other wives for a consistent
and regular time of prayer for their husbands. "Okay, Lord," she
prayed, "if you bring the women, I'll do it."

The next day Tami received a call from her friend Cindy. Just
before they ended their conversation, Cindy asked Tami if she'd
like to get together to pray for their husbands. "I nearly dropped the
phone!" said Tami. "I'd never seen God work so fast!" Talk about an
answer to prayer in the nick of time—this was it." We looked at our
calendars and chose Friday mornings as our time to pray together.
"Wives in Prayer" was born that first meeting. Soon their friend
Caryn joined them, and then other women were calling, eager to
be part of this unique group of praying wives.

"I've seen God take my prayers and those of like-minded women
and answer them beyond anything we hoped for or imagined," Tami
said, still amazed at how much has occurred by the power of prayer.

No longer does Tami put the Bible at the foot of their bed as a
reminder. Dan's faith is flourishing. Each morning before leaving
for work, Dan reads his Bible for direction, wisdom, and strength
for his day. Tami watches in awe…from the sidelines.

"It's exciting to see how marriages have been changed when wives
pray," Tami said. "One woman's husband had been diagnosed with
cancer. As a result it appeared they'd not be able to have children.
We prayed Scripture prayers for him, specifically that God would
heal his body and bless him and his wife with the ability to conceive. At the end of the year, his cancer was in remission and she
was pregnant."

She also told of a husband who was belligerent, emotionally
unstable, and verbally and mentally abusive to his wife and family.
"Their children asked their mother if they could leave because life
in their home was so miserable," said Tami. "The woman felt God
was asking her to stay—and pray. She began a prayer group in her
office." Since these women have been praying together, she's seen
real changes in her husband. His emotions are more stable, he's nicer
to be around, and he is now open to Christian counseling. She even
admitted she's falling in love with him all over again. Not long ago
they celebrated their twentieth anniversary.

"My husband is now much more interested in prayer," added Tami. "We pray together before our day begins, with our daughters before they go to school, and at night before we go to bed. God has blessed our family financially, spiritually, and relationally in more ways than I can count. I *know* God answers our prayers!"

A successful marriage requires falling in love many times,
always with the same person.

Mignon McLaughlin

Is there something in your life that not only disturbs you, but makes you a disturbance to others? If so, it is always something you cannot handle yourself. "Then those who went before warned [the blind man] that he should be quiet; but he cried out all the more..." (Luke 18:39). Be persistent with your disturbance until you get face to face with the Lord Himself. Don't defy common sense. To sit calmly by, instead of creating a disturbance, serves only to deify our common sense. When Jesus asks what we want him to do for us about the incredible problem that is confronting us, remember that he doesn't work in common-sense ways, but only in supernatural ways.

Oswald Chambers,
My Utmost for His Highest

Never Too Late

Whatever you ask for in prayer,
believe that you have received it, and it will be yours.
MARK 11:24

"I tend to be controlling by nature," said my friend Barbara as we sat together sipping tea at our favorite cafe. "But I'm working on letting go," she added. "I've learned so much in the last few years. Forty-seven seems a little old to be learning parenting skills. Especially since my three children are adults," she added playfully. "But I'm their mother, and I want to change some of the ways I relate to them. I'm not as close as I'd like to be, especially with my second son."

Barbara and I had recently become acquainted and were enjoying the discovery of how much we had in common. I have three grown children, as well. And, like Barbara, I had been divorced from a man who left our family for another woman and subsequently married her. Barbara's voice broke into my thoughts.

"After my husband left, I was filled with anger. But I covered it by controlling everything and everyone around me." Like so many women in the same situation, Barbara needed to run a household, take a job outside her home, and meet her children's needs without a partner's help.

"The emotional area is probably where I felt the greatest challenge," she said. "Helping them develop as persons was so difficult, especially when our only quality time together was at nine or ten o'clock at night when we were all tired and there were a billion things to do before the next day."

I could relate to that too. I remember one evening shortly after my husband had moved out. My older daughter needed to talk to me, but I was so focused on my own pain I was only half present. When I think of it now, I can only imagine how insecure and frightened she must have felt. She could no longer count on her father, and now she must have felt she couldn't count on me either.

Barbara paused for a moment, and I noticed her eyes mist as she reflected on her son Kurt. "From the time he was a little boy, he had tantrums that absolutely baffled me. By the time he was a young adult, his feelings were erupting all over the house. He slammed doors, threw things, and whenever I approached him about it, he'd keep me away by creating a scene that was so explosive I'd back off."

Barbara realized that she had to set limits for her sake and for the sake of her other two children. "If we were to have a healthy home, I could no longer allow Kurt to manipulate us for his own needs," she said.

Shortly after realizing that, she told him if he wanted to remain a member of the household, there were certain duties and responsibilities that went along with the privilege of being part of the family. "If he didn't do them," she said, "then I would interpret this to mean he didn't care to live with us. I then asked him to put away a number of his items that had been cluttering up our common living areas and to get himself out of bed for school in the mornings. These were activities I'd been asking him to do for weeks with no visible response from him." This time there was an ultimatum. Complete the job by noon or move out. By twelve o'clock he'd done nothing. She went to his room and told him he had made his choice. "Pack your things and be out by one o'clock," she told him. Kurt looked at Barbara in complete disbelief. Immediately he backed down and wanted to talk things out.

"I said I'd be happy to talk, but that wouldn't change the one o'clock deadline. We both became emotional. I told him I loved him, and that I wanted to work things out. But I also knew I couldn't let him use his tears to manipulate me one more time."

At one, Barbara said goodbye. "I had no idea where he would go or what he was going to do. I had to be willing to never see Kurt again," she said, "because when you set limits and release a child under those circumstances, you don't know if he'll ever come back to you. It was so hard. He was only 17. It was definitely the lowest point in my life as a mother."

That night Barbara learned that Kurt had moved in with his father. For the next nine months, they had almost no contact except for a family gathering at the home of Barbara's parents. Later that year—one full year after he'd moved out of his mother's house—Kurt asked to come home. "At that point he thanked me for having confronted him and for holding the line," said Barbara.

Now that Kurt is an adult working and living on his own in another city, Barbara said their relationship is more cordial and more giving. "But there is still a ways to go," she said. "I know I can't change the past. I can't undo my divorce from his father. I can't replace my temperament. But I am willing to grow and change. And I know God is with me in this. I pray daily for his guidance."

As I drove home that morning, I thought about Barbara's last words, "God is with me in this." I was reminded of the day I broke down at a prayer meeting at church and asked what I could do to restore my wayward son to me. A dear older woman hurried across the room, sat down beside me, and slipped her arm around my shoulder. "Your parenting in the flesh is over," she said softly. "It's time to parent him in the Spirit. Pray for your son, and trust God to do what you cannot do. He will!" she added confidently.

I was set free that day. The God who reconciled his relationship to his children through the sacrifice of Jesus Christ would surely give me, and all mothers and fathers who asked for it, the grace to reconcile with our adult children.

I knew I couldn't rewrite the past, and I couldn't shut the door on it either. But I also knew Jesus could! He mends broken hearts and broken relationships. I learned in the nick of time that it is never too late to start over.

Swallow your pride occasionally. It's not fattening.

Frank Tyger

Some Ride

You will pray to [God], and he will hear you.
JOB 22:27

My husband and I spent a week in Dallas, Texas, attending a book convention. On the last day, we hired a driver to take us from our hotel to the Dallas/Fort Worth Airport in a fancy town car. His service was more expensive than riding a shuttle bus, but we didn't mind. We were in a hurry, and we were hot. The city had been hit with one of the worst heat waves in recent history.

An hour later, as we pulled into the airport and parked near the sign marked "American Airlines," I was suddenly aware of how the heat and stress were affecting everyone around us. Travelers were short-tempered, and airport personnel wiped their brows as they hoisted heavy luggage onto conveyor belts. Horns honked and angry bus and taxi drivers swung in and out of small spaces as though they owned the street.

Charles and I jumped out of the car, eager to check our bags and take refuge in the cool interior of the airport. "Hold on a moment, folks," our driver, Scotty, called as he pulled our suitcases from the trunk. "I'd like to take a minute to pray for you." He told us how much he enjoyed meeting us and discovering that we loved the Lord as much as he did. "Let's ask him to bless your journey." He also asked for our prayers for his new chauffeuring business.

I was so disarmed by his vulnerability that I wasn't sure what to do. As he reached for our shoulders, I got teary-eyed. What might

people think of three adults holding onto one another and praying out loud in front of an international airport in broad daylight?

My husband nudged me with an elbow. I joined in without
another thought to what was going on around us. Scotty, Charles,
and I huddled together, arms linked like a coach and two players
for the Dallas Cowboys. Scotty led us in a short prayer, and then we
said one for him. We hugged even tighter, exchanged business cards
in case we ever returned to Dallas, and turned to leave.

I looked over my shoulder as Scotty walked around to the driver's side. He waved and smiled. "See you in heaven, if not before!" I
called, surprising myself. A few people stared at me, but by then I
didn't care. What a send-off! I couldn't have planned a better way
to end our glorious week in Dallas.

God sent Scotty to us and maybe us to him. He chastened me in
the nick of time or I might have missed this opportunity to put my
self-centered thoughts aside and enter into prayer with a "brother
in Christ."

The difference between ordinary and extraordinary is that little extra.
Jimmy Johnson

Where to Now?

LORD, you are my God; I will exalt you and praise your name,
for in perfect faithfulness you have done wonderful things,
things planned long ago.
ISAIAH 25:1

Month after month Pharaoh either refused to grant Moses permission to lead the Israelites out or granted it and then changed his mind. This time was no exception. Right after they departed, Pharaoh commanded and led his army to follow them and bring them back. Exhausted, afraid, and filled with worry, the Israelites hurled complaints at Moses when they saw the Egyptian army pursuing them. After all, Moses was their leader. Why wasn't he doing anything to save them from certain death?

Then Moses prayed, and God told him to have the people continue to move on. So the people trudged forward, with the army hot on their heels. Soon they came to the edge of the Red Sea. What now? They were stuck. There was no escape. If they kept moving they'd drown. If they turned back, the Egyptian army would capture them. Only God could rescue them!

Imagine the pandemonium that broke out—children clinging to parents, old men and women fearing they'd be left behind, strong men overcome by their inability to save their families, women crying for their loved ones. Some may have cursed Moses or even God, while others fell on their faces in prayer for Jehovah to intervene.

Moses must have felt an overwhelming burden for the people, and yet he held on to his faith and trust.

At the brink of disaster, he stepped forward and proclaimed: "Do not be afraid. Stand firm and you will see the deliverance the LORD will bring you today. The Egyptians you see today you will never see again. The LORD will fight for you; you need only to be still" (Exodus 14:13-14). What courage it took to "stand firm" with an army bearing down on them and the Red Sea in front of them. The group of followers trembled with fear.

In the nick of time, God came through—giving Moses the exact steps to take:

> Tell the Israelites to move on. Raise your staff and stretch out your hand over the sea to divide the water so that the Israelites can go through the sea on dry ground. I will harden the hearts of the Egyptians so that they will go in after them. And I will gain glory through Pharaoh and all his army, through his chariots and his horsemen. The Egyptians will know that I am the LORD when I gain glory through Pharaoh, his chariots and his horsemen (verses 16-18).

Then the angel of God who was traveling in front of the Israelites moved behind them, and the pillar of cloud in front also moved to the rear, obscuring the view of the Egyptians. Moses stretched out his hand over the sea, and in that instant, the Red Sea was parted by a strong wind and dry land was exposed. Walls of water were on the right and on the left. All night the Israelites crossed over the dry sea bed. Imagine the shouts of praise that ascended to their God in heaven!

But God didn't stop there. He caused great confusion among the Egyptians and jammed the wheels of their chariots. He then commanded Moses to stretch out his hand over the sea once again so the waters once again would flow. The Egyptians with their chariots and the horsemen who had foolishly tried to follow were drowned. Not one person in Pharaoh's army survived. In one mighty act, God wiped out Israel's enemy (verse 28).

And all the Israelites believed what Moses had been teaching them, having seen and experienced this supernatural event for themselves.

I had therefore to remove knowledge, in order to make room for belief.
Immanuel Kant

Stress Overturned

Come to me, all you who are weary and burdened,
and I will give you rest.
MATTHEW 11:28

"My husband, Allen, and I hit many financial hurdles in the past few years," Miralee shared. "But the most recent episode brought its own truckload of stress. It seemed it was going to bury us." The couple had put their house on the market three different times over the past four years with no success. "We did so again, but nothing appeared to have changed. I was nearing desperation," Miralee said. "But I made the commitment to pray until I sensed a breakthrough in my spirit. Allen and I also decided to give a generous 'breakthrough offering' to our church. We couldn't afford it, but we followed the scriptural principle of giving over and above our tithes, asking that the windows of heaven be opened for us."

Two weeks passed, and Miralee and Allen continued to press into the Lord, praying for a buyer to purchase their home. "One evening I hit a low," said Miralee, "which was unusual for me and my upbeat personality. I cried out to God, asking for mercy and a renewed sense of hope. I praised him and then settled into a time of listening in my spirit. Within moments I heard, very softly, these words: 'It will be sold in one week.' *One week?* I thought. *How could that be?* No one had even come to look at the property."

She wondered if maybe God meant that within a week someone would view the house and then start the purchase process. "Two days later a friend called. His relatives were flying into town and looking for a house to buy. He believed our home in the country was ideal. He asked if they could drop by."

Miralee agreed. Upon arriving, the husband and wife spent several hours walking the property and talking. They returned for another visit the following day. "That evening they called with an offer, and the next day we signed earnest money papers," said Miralee. "A total of six days had passed from the time the Lord told me 'one week.'"

What did they gain from this experience? "That God is big enough to handle anything that comes our way, no matter how stressful or urgent!" Miralee exclaimed. She added that she now listens more and asks less. "I truly want to know what the Lord has to say rather than simply pouring out my needs and walking away."

God showed His faithfulness when the situation looked hopeless. "Since then we've faced other difficult circumstances," said Miralee, "but my stress has been so much lower than it was with the sale of our house. I'm able to look back at God's awesome intervention and know he hears me, and that his mercy and power are more than enough to meet all of our needs. And that's the case even when he chooses to meet them in the nick of time."

There are things known,
and there are things unknown.
And in-between are the doors.

Jim Morrison

Trust Me

Take delight in the LORD,
and he will give you the desires of your heart.
PSALM 37:4

Jenna stared at the large box with a silver ribbon and the smaller one wrapped in yellow tissue. Both were stacked on the edge of the dining room table. A bouquet of red and white tea roses lay beside them. She picked up the gift card tucked between the stems. "Happy 13th, honey," she read. "I'm sorry to miss your special day. We'll celebrate together when I get home. Won't be long now. Love, Mom."

Jenna felt her eyes blur with tears. "Sorry to miss your day." She'd heard those words often. The day of the mother–daughter banquet at church when she was seven. The evening of the parent–student open house last September. The night earlier in the year when Jenna had made her mother a cake and decorated the house as a surprise for her thirty-eighth birthday...but her mom had missed the plane at New Orleans and didn't make it home till after midnight. She hadn't been home for her own birthday, so why should Jenna expect her to be home for hers?

"Open your presents!" Jenna's little sister, Meg, pleaded, hopping from one foot to the other.

Jenna forced a smile and swiped at a tear rolling down her cheek. She looked at the beautiful cake with pink frosting sitting on the glass plate as her father carried it in from the kitchen and placed it in the center of the table. It looked like the one she'd seen at Dessert Cart. Fancy white letters spelled out "HAPPY BIRTHDAY, JENNA" and beneath it was "Proverbs 3:5" in smaller letters. Ever since she could remember, it had been her family's custom to put a Scripture on each birthday cake. After everyone sang "Happy Birthday," her parents would read the passage out loud. Jenna had never heard of any other family doing anything like it. That made it even more special. And she liked their tradition of having a private celebration with only the immediate family on each person's birthday.

For special days like this one, they'd have a big party with friends and relatives later in the week. Finally, at 13, Jenna could say she was a teenager!

Her dad interrupted her thoughts.

"What's wrong, honey? Did I choose the wrong cake? I saw you looking at one like it last week."

"No. It's beautiful. Honest." Jenna gulped hard and pushed back the tears that clouded her eyes again.

Meg continued her impatient dancing from one foot to the other.

"I promise I'll open my presents," Jenna said, as she picked up her sister and sat her on the table next to the cake. "But let's blow out the candles first, okay? You can help. And I want Dad to read the Scripture."

Jenna counted to three, nodded at Meg, and they blew out the flames in one puff. After having cake, Jenna opened her presents. Then her dad opened the Bible to Proverbs chapter 3, verse 5. "Trust in the LORD with all your heart," he read, "and lean not on your own understanding."

He closed the Bible and looked at Jenna, reaching over to tilt her chin upward with his hand. "Mom picked out this passage," he said. "It was important to her *this* year especially, now that you're a young woman. You'll be facing new decisions and making new choices."

Jenna felt her heart beat faster. *Mom picked this out? She doesn't come home for my birthday, but she...she makes sure the right verse is on the cake?*

Jenna's dad continued. "Trust the Lord—always," he said, "in every situation. Lean on *his* understanding, especially in tough times. He loves you—even more than we do."

"Thanks, Dad," she said without a smile.

"Is something the matter?" her father asked, as he slipped an arm around her shoulder.

"Yes!" Jenna erupted and pulled away. Anger poured over the room like hot lava. "Why *isn't* Mom here? She's *never* home when *I* want her—when I *need* her!" She sobbed.

"It's not easy, I know." Her dad tried to comfort her. Then he looked at her straight in the eyes. "Your mother is a news correspondent," he said, emphasizing each word. "She is the mother you have."

Jenna said she was taken aback by his directness.

Then his voice softened. "All of us live with the uncertainty of her assignments and her schedule. But we agreed as a family that her work is important and we'd support her. You may not understand now, but someday you will."

"You're right, Dad. I don't understand," Jenna snapped. "How come she can go to Bangladesh or San Francisco, but she can't be home on her daughter's thirteenth birthday? Or for parent night at school? Or...?"

"Suddenly nothing seemed important," Jenna shared. "I ran upstairs to my bedroom," she said. "At that moment I didn't care about the new skates from Dad or the angora mittens and hat from Meg."

All she wanted was for her mother to be there, to bake her a cake, to sing "Happy Birthday," to watch her blow out the candles, and to take her skating like she used to do.

Jenna said she grabbed the phone and dialed her best friend's number. "Reen, I'm so glad you're home."

"Hey, happy birthday. Today's the *real* day, isn't it? Can't wait for your party at the ice rink on Saturday."

"Me too," Jenna said, trying to sound happy. "Speaking of the ice rink, guess what? Dad got me skates..."

"Cool! No more 'boxes with blades,'" Reenie joked. "But you don't *sound* excited. What's up?"

"Mom didn't make it home—*again*."

"Oh, I'm sorry. I know you were looking forward to it. But, hey, girl, it's not like she's gone *all* the time."

"Seems like it to me."

"How can you say that?"

Some friend. She's taking Mom's side, Jenna thought.

"Remember when she helped you with your geography collage for Mr. Dickson's class? If you hadn't been invited to go to Vermont with your mom, your project wouldn't have been nearly as good. And what about..."

Reenie's voice faded as Jenna's thoughts wandered back to the trip to Vermont. She'd even got to tap a maple tree for syrup. And then she remembered the time she and her mother went ice-skating for the first time. They laughed till their sides ached as they wobbled around the edge of the rink together. And her mother had been at her side the night Jenna was rushed to the hospital with pneumonia. "Nothing could keep me away," her mother had whispered over and over.

"...And remember the day you and your mom and I planted rose bushes in that little plot in your yard?" Reenie asked, breaking into Jenna's thoughts.

"I do. Thanks, Reenie. Gotta go. See you Saturday. Hugs."

"Hugs back. Bye."

Jenna put down the phone and fell back onto her bed. "Oh God," she prayed, "I'm sorry for being so selfish. I know Mom loves me. Please help me get over this bad mood I'm in." Later she awoke to the sound of a soft knock on her bedroom door. It was Meg reminding her it was time to go out for dinner. As Jenna walked toward the door she caught sight of the photo of her mother on the dresser. "Kathleen Taylor Ackerman—correspondent," she said, mimicking the way her mother was introduced on television. Suddenly she felt calm. The words her dad had read washed over her like a spring rain. "Do not lean on your own understanding." "You're right, Lord," she said aloud. "I don't understand Mom sometimes. But I love her, and I know she loves me. I have to trust you." Jenna took a deep breath, grabbed a sweater, and headed for the door. The Lord had answered her prayer in the nick of time. She and her dad and sister would have a great time celebrating her birthday, and they'd talk to Mom later via Skype.

All I have seen teaches me to trust the creator for all I have not seen.
Ralph Waldo Emerson

Auto Heaven

A faithful person will be richly blessed.
PROVERBS 28:20

My sporty 1978 Toyota Celica with the convenient hatchback and chrome wheels had taken me up and down the coast of California and in and out of parking lots for 14 years. We'd become the best of friends. But it was clear my dear auto was telling me it was time for her to go to a better place. So I released her one day after she collapsed in the middle of the boulevard in front of the apartment house where I lived.

I broke the news to my husband when he returned from work that day. Then he broke the news to me that he'd been thinking of replacing his 10-year-old car since it was behaving poorly. We had a good laugh and then sobered when we realized that the bankruptcy we'd gone through five years before would likely prevent us from getting a loan for one new car, let alone two.

Times had been really tough for us the last few years, and though we were climbing back, we still had a hill or two to scale before achieving a sound credit rating. We decided to replace my vehicle first since Charles's car was still running. This time we'd settle for a used model.

The following Sunday afternoon we made a list of dealerships to visit in our area, but we never got beyond the first one, located just a mile from our home. We walked into the showroom, and a friendly salesman greeted us. We quickly discovered he was the sales manager. I'd decided ahead of time that I would be completely aboveboard when the time came to reveal our financial situation. No hedging or pretending or lying. Just the facts. Then we'd sit back and pray for mercy.

We talked about pre-owned vehicles, but instead of taking us to the used car lot, the manager led us to a fleet of *new* stick-shift Ford Escorts free of extras except for power steering and radios. The price was right: $10,000 each to get out the door. At that price, we might be able to buy both cars we needed.

I stared at a station wagon in light-blue. My husband was enamored with a white sedan. The longer I looked, the more convinced I was that my name was stamped on the driver's door, invisible to anyone but me—and God. *Lord, are you telling me this car is mine?* I prayed silently.

My heart quickened. My mouth went dry. The salesman spoke up, telling us why cars from the budget fleet would be a much wiser investment than used autos. We agreed though we're no experts when it comes to such matters.

Charles and I looked at each other, smiled, and then nodded as we followed the manager into his cubicle. The moment had come—the moment of truth. I opened my purse, pulled out our bankruptcy papers, and plopped them on his desk. "Sir, we have a confession to make, and we want to get it out before we go any further." He looked at me with wide eyes. I told him what happened to our finances, and how we'd had no other way out of our trouble. "However," I continued, "we both have jobs now and steady monthly incomes. I feel certain we can make car payments. We just need a little help, someone to take a chance on us."

"Excuse me," said the manager. "I'll be right back."

My heart lurched as I saw him walk out the door. I was certain he'd return with bad news. But when he came back with a smile on his face, my pulse jumped. "Follow me," he said. And we did, right into the finance director's office. The manager then placed a hand on the desk and said without hesitation. "These fine folks have had some bad luck. They deserve a second chance. Give them the loans they need, and I'll take full responsibility for the decision."

He shook our hands with vigor. "Enjoy your brand-new cars," he said. "I hope they serve you well for years to come."

And that's exactly what happened—for 13 years. Once more God showed us that his timing and his plans are always perfect, even when they come to pass in the nick of time.

In any situation, the best thing you can do is the right thing.
Theodore Roosevelt

In God's Arms

God is not human, that he should lie,
not a human being, that he should change his mind.
NUMBERS 23:19

The apostles faced some tough times after Jesus returned to his Father in heaven. Members of the new church in Jerusalem gave alms to the poor without complaint, but the flock grew so quickly that some of the widows were overlooked. Their friends complained to Peter and the others, so the band of 12 disciples called the entire church together to clarify what was really important.

"It would not be right for us to neglect the ministry of the word of God in order to wait on tables. Brothers and sisters, choose seven men from among you who are known to be full of the Spirit and wisdom. We will turn this responsibility over to them and will give our attention to prayer and the ministry of the word" (Acts 6:2-4).

Everyone agreed this was a good plan, so they chose seven men to take charge of distributing the gifts of the people to those who were in real need. First they selected a man named Stephen, who was filled with faith and the Spirit of God. Along with Stephen, Philip and five other good men made up the seven. The apostles laid their hands on their heads and prayed for them, establishing that they would do the important work of caring for the poor.

Stephen took on more than mere good works. He preached the gospel of Christ with such power that every man and woman who heard him felt the truth, and many came to salvation. But opposition arose against Stephen's views. The dissenters couldn't withstand the wisdom the Holy Spirit gave to Stephen. So these men falsely accused him of heresy. Stephen was captured and ordered to appear before the great Jewish council called the Sanhedrin. Then false witnesses testified against him. One of the spokesmen said, "This fellow never stops speaking against this holy place and against the law. For we have heard him say that this Jesus of Nazareth will destroy this place and change the customs Moses handed down to us" (Acts 6:13-14).

"Are these charges true?" asked the high priest.

Stephen stood up to answer, and all eyes fixed on his shining face (verse 15). Then he spoke of the great things God had done for his people of Israel over the years, how he had called Abraham to go forth into a new land and given them great men, including Joseph, Moses, and the prophets. He showed them how the Israelites had not been faithful to God who had given them such blessings. Then he wrapped up his message:

> You stiff-necked people! Your hearts and ears are still uncir-
> cumcised. You are just like your ancestors: You always resist
> the Holy Spirit! Was there ever a prophet your ancestors
> did not persecute? They even killed those who predicted
> the coming of the Righteous One. And now you have
> betrayed and murdered him—you who have received the
> law that was given through angels but have not obeyed it
> (Acts 7:51-53).

The members of the Sanhedrin rose up in fury and gnashed their teeth at the brazenness of this man. But Stephen, full of the Holy Spirit, gazed up. "Look...I see heaven open and the Son of Man standing at the right hand of God" (verse 56). The people covered their ears, yelled at the top of their voices, and rushed at Stephen. They dragged him out of the city and hurled stones at him. As the storm of rocks came at him, Stephen prayed aloud, "'Lord Jesus, receive my spirit.' Then he fell on his knees and cried out, 'Lord, do not hold this sin against them.' When he had said this, he fell asleep" (verses 59-60). In the nick of time he was safe in the arms of God.

It is truer to say that martyrs create faith more than faith creates martyrs.

Miguel de Unamuno

More Great Harvest House Books by
Karen O'Connor

365 Reasons Why Gettin' Old Ain't So Bad

365 Senior Moments You'd Rather Forget

Addicted to Shopping and Other Issues
Women Have with Money

Gettin' Old Ain't for Wimps

Gettin' Old Ain't for Wimps! (gift edition)

The Golden Years Ain't for Wimps

Grandkids Say the Cutest Things

Grandma, You Rock!

It's Taken Years to Get This Old

The Upside of Downsizing

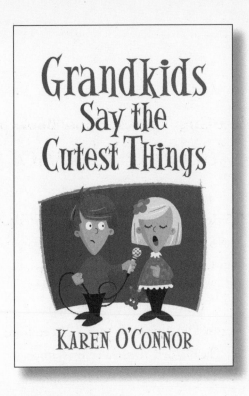

Grandkids Say the Cutest Things
Words to Warm Your Heart

Grandkids are amazing! Gathering a charming collection of their quotes and antics, humorist and bestselling author Karen O'Connor hopes they'll brighten your day. These vignettes celebrate the candid comments and honest observations the young make about life, God, grandparents, and more.

You'll smile, chuckle, and even laugh out loud as you read these entertaining bits that are sure to remind you of the many cute things your grandkids have shared.

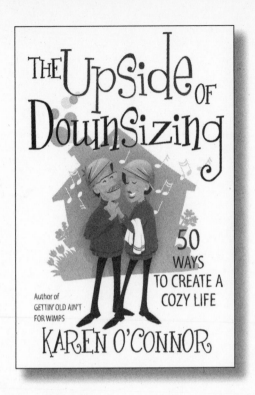

The Upside of Downsizing
Streamlining Your Life

Ready to tackle the clutter? Wondering what to do with the extra space since the kids have moved out? Bestselling author Karen O'Connor offers encouragement and suggestions for upsizing your happiness and downsizing stress. Each short chapter includes inspiring quotes, biblical wisdom, and practical advice to help you...

- get the most out of this new life phase
- simplify and winnow responsibilities and possessions
- rediscover the joys of life without children and teens

Now is a great time to develop your interests and create a vibrant, energetic lifestyle.